The Glory of Christ in His Church

The Glory of Christ in His Church

Samuel J. Stoesz

CHRISTIAN PUBLICATIONS, INC.
CAMP HILL, PENNSYLVANIA

Christian Publications
3825 Hartzdale Drive, Camp Hill, PA 17011

Faithful, biblical publishing since 1883

ISBN: 0–87509–569–0
© 1994 by Christian Publications
All rights reserved
Printed in the United States of America

94   95   96   97   98   5   4   3   2

Cover: Robert Baddorf

#31600869

Contents

Preface

*U*nderstanding My Church, published in 1968, was my attempt to acquaint Christian and Missionary Alliance laypeople with our church's biblical and historical purposes. I wrote it at the request of the church's National Education Committee. My *Church and Membership Awareness*, a training manual for new members, issued in 1974, had a similar objective.

The Glory of Christ in His Church, requested by Richard Weber Bailey, Vice President, Church Ministries, is designed as an ecclesiology for church leaders. As professor of systematic theology and pastoral studies at Nyack College and, later, Canadian Theological Seminary, I found no text that adequately set forth Alliance thought on this important subject. George P. Pardington's *Outline Studies in Christian Doctrine,* published posthumously in 1916 from his teaching notes as professor at the Missionary Training Institute, offered valuable insights, but then The Christian and Missionary Alliance was a transdenominational missionary society, not a church. Since 1916 no thorough description has been attempted.

While this book does not assume official sanction, I have been privileged to work alongside the Church Ministries staff, who have taken time to read the manuscript and offer suggestions. Final drafts of my work have been examined by selected readers: Arnold L. Cook, President,

1

The Christian and Missionary Alliance in Canada; Robert W. Battles, long-time Alliance pastor and former secretary of The Christian and Missionary Alliance; John S. Sawin, former missionary, pastor, archivist and a coauthor of the C&MA centennial history, *All for Jesus*; Jack F. Shepherd, retired Alliance educator and missiologist; and Robert P. Turner, prominent Alliance pastor. For their valuable help and support I am deeply grateful.

I am indebted as well to David E. Schroeder, president of Nyack College and to David R. Enlow, former associate editor of *Alliance Life,* for their editorial assistance. I want also to thank the office staff of the Southeastern District for their help.

Finally, this opportunity to attempt the formidable I owe to the confidence and inspiration of Richard W. Bailey. His gracious and kind encouragement made this writing possible.

Samuel J. Stoesz
Orlando, Florida
May, 1994

Foreword

Over the centuries pallbearers have been standing in line ready to carry the church to her burial. Friends from within and foes from without have attacked the church. Her enemies protest her bells that disturb their Sunday morning sleep. Others lament her tax-free status.

Some more aggressive adversaries dynamite and bulldoze her temples. But even in Russia the church has emerged triumphant from 70 years of Communism, attesting once again to Christ's resolve to "build My church."

Recently there has been a plethora of books addressing the church. But one from the perspective of The Christian and Missionary Alliance as a missionary denomination is long overdue. Samuel J. Stoesz, well schooled in theology and steeped in Alliance history, draws from the writings of our founder, A.B. Simpson. He sets the record straight.

Contrary to the opinion of many, Simpson had a very strong ecclesiology. Much of the theology of his time focused on the attributes and works of God, but it was strangely silent on the purposes of God. This book gives us a solid biblical theology of mission.

Throughout his ministry first as a pastor and particularly as a seminary professor, the church was one of Dr. Stoesz's favorite themes. He delivered his soul with passion on the subject. He lamented the shoddy ecclesiology that characterized too many churches. His earlier little volume, *Understanding My Church,* has been used widely to help Alliance people understand their own roots.

In a day when even the professed friends of the church are unconsciously undermining her foundation, questioning her authority and diluting her mission and message, this book could not be more timely.

Arnold L. Cook, President
The Christian and Missionary Alliance in Canada

1

The Church Unfolds

*T*he church of Jesus Christ is unique. As woman was created from man, so the church has been created from Christ (Ephesians 5:25–30). From the beginning of time it has been bound up in the purpose of God (Colossians 1:17–20). One cannot read the Acts, the Letters or the Revelation without realizing that God designed the church to be above every other agency or institution. Albert B. Simpson observed: "[The church] is the only divine society on earth, the only institution that is essential, eternal and will survive the wreck of time and the dissolution of the present age. Let us understand her high calling and, oh, let her be true to it!"[1]

The church is a glorious revelation because Jesus Christ is the foundation of the church and its Lord (Matthew

16:18; Colossians 1:18). He who sacrificed Himself for the church will return for her (1 Thessalonians 4:13–18) and with her will establish His dominion on earth (1 Corinthians 15:24–28). He calls the church His bride, who is to reign as joint heir with Him (Romans 8:17). Until then He is head over "everything for the church" (Ephesians 1:22). This "everything" includes kings and other rulers and leaders and all things of this world or of worlds to come (Ephesians 1:21).

These truths, as comprehensive and glorious as they are, can obscure what is of immediate importance if we are to assimilate their meaning for us. After providing insight to the Ephesian believers into God's plan for the church and the way Christ has designed and gifted His church for ministry, Paul asks these believers in Ephesus to examine the main purpose behind it all. They need to gain strength and maturity by thinking alike about Christ and His fullness in order that together they might "become more and more in every way like Christ who is the Head of His body, the Church" (Ephesians 4:11–16 LB). Christ alone is the key to the believers' fuller comprehension of their opportunity in life and the meaning of their relationship to Him and His church.

To experience the fullness of Christ, therefore, is the church's highest calling, and to this believers ought to be true. Christ Himself is to be their focus and sense of direction! And although this comprehensive and glorious revelation of the church provides the context, the secret of divine fullness is in Christ Himself and the union believers can experience with Him. No wonder Paul expresses such soaring enthusiasm for the church in his impromptu prayer: "Now to him who is able to do immeasurably more than all we ask or imagine, according to his power that is at work within us, to him be glory in the church and in Christ Jesus throughout all generations, for ever and ever! Amen" (Ephesians 3:20–21).

Like facets of a diamond, the Scriptures give us a variety of perspectives regarding the church. To look at some of them is to realize how central Christ must be to our understanding of the church and how God has designed the church to reflect Christ's fullness.

The Church Is Christ's Body

The Holy Spirit working through the corporate church as Christ's body can be understood only by spiritual illumination. A.B. Simpson wrote: "The same Spirit who wrought in Christ [God] has given to the church to perform her work of love and power. This is what the Master meant when He said,'Anyone who has faith in me will do what I have been doing. He will do even greater things than these, because I am going to the Father'(John 14:12). The Holy Spirit in us is the same Holy Spirit who wrought in Christ."[2]

It is difficult to imagine any miracle greater than bringing to life Lazarus, who had been four days dead. Qualitatively, we cannot do greater miracles. But who can doubt that the followers of Christ, as they worked the past nearly 20 centuries within and supported by the corporate church, have outpaced in quantity the miracles Jesus wrought during His three and a half years on earth? Work done in union with Christ through the organic provision of His body has been indeed greater than Christ's ministry while He was on earth.

When Jesus returned to the Father He sent the Holy Spirit and the New Testament church was born. From that point on, it would not be what individual persons accomplished but what responsible members of the body of Christ, complementing each other, accomplished. This pivotal position God has given the church has nothing in its equal. Personal fulfillment must be seen primarily in terms of corporate fulfillment.

In the Likeness of Christ

Sanctified communal service in the organic unity of the church is selfless. It glorifies Christ and seeks to build His body. Self-fulfillment is assuredly a wonderful blessing, but such blessing comes by giving, not by receiving; in ministering, not by being ministered to. Our Lord exemplified this selfless giving. Speaking of Himself He said, "The Son of man did not come to be served, but to serve, and to give his life as a ransom for many" (Mark 10:45).

Spiritual gifts become most effective when they are related to the body, the church. Thus they open honest relationships. They encourage truth spoken in love. They provide fellowship with Christ and with others in creative and self-sustaining ways. All of these benefits come from a total commitment to Christ and His body. They come as we corporately and personally seek for Christ's fullness.

The church's glorious identity is in her being the body of Christ, representing His fullness (Ephesians 1:22–23; 1 Corinthians 12:27). It is the body through which Christ, now in heaven, does His work on earth. For this reason Paul challenged the members of the church at Rome to offer their bodies as "living sacrifices, holy and pleasing to God" (Romans 12:1). Paul calls it their "spiritual act of worship." Such living would be in bold contrast to the world. It would provide them a fresh new way of thinking. It would demonstrate God's will as "good, pleasing and perfect" (12:2).

The apostle follows his challenge with a warning to church members not to think of themselves more highly than they should. Rather, in sober judgment they were to regard themselves in terms of whole body involvement: "Just as each of us has one body with many members, and these members do not all have the same function, so in Christ we who are many form one body, and each member belongs to all the others" (12:3–5). Total commitment to the body begins with total commitment to Christ. This is not a mere option but a new and different disposition of the mind. Such consecrated living is needed both for the function of the body as a whole and for every member to find in the body his own identity and personal fulfillment. To be content with anything less is to miss what Christlikeness is all about.

Organically United with Christ

Paul learned through his conversion experience that marginal living was fruitless and unchallenging. He had recognized in the believers he persecuted a commitment he had tried to match with Judaistic zeal. Apparently even prior to his conversion Paul recognized these believers as representing an organic union, as being "the church." To the Galatians he recounts his faith pilgrimage by beginning: "You have heard of my previous way of life in Judaism, how intensely I persecuted the church of God and tried to destroy it" (Galatians 1:13).

The church's divine origin, its identity with Jesus Christ and Jesus' glorified, authoritative, powerful presence within it overwhelmed Paul and readied him for repentance. It was not so much the witness of a particular individual—not even the martyr Stephen—that convicted Paul as it was the witness that came through the organic oneness of the church. Christ's own living presence produces the church by the Holy Spirit and ministers through it. As Head of the body He regenerates the cells, fitting them with His nature. He then by His Spirit works through the church, His body, to "convict the world of guilt in regard to sin and righteousness and judgment" (John 16:8).

Paul's conversion on the road to Damascus elicited a statement from the glorified Christ that verified the church as His body: "Saul, Saul, why do you persecute me?" (Acts 9:4).

When Paul asked the identity of the voice, Jesus answered, "I am Jesus, whom you are persecuting." When Paul later retells the experience, he has Jesus saying, "I am Jesus of Nazareth, whom you are persecuting" (Acts 22:8). The incarnate Jesus of Nazareth now had a new incarnate identity in His ascended enthronement: the church.

The church's glory is in its identity and union with Christ, not in its own virtue. The church's mission in the world comes out of its divine origin and divine life. The

9

church is not merely an extension of Christ's incarnation, for Christ remains distinct in His resurrection and ascended glory. The church nevertheless represents Christ and His global intentions (Colossians 1:25–27). The church witnesses to the world by incarnating Christ's own life into flesh-and-blood people who form a body-life community on this earth. The church's calling is a mission, even as Christ came into the world to save sinners (John 3:17; 12:47). This mission comes through an organic unity. For Paul, it became a part of his vision.

The Local Church and the Universal

"The body of Christ" is a metaphor used in the universal sense (Ephesians 1:22; Colossians 1:18), but it is only meaningful when expressed locally. Of the 115 times the word *church* is used in the New Testament, local churches are in focus 96 times. Each individual church must view itself as part of the universal church and seek unity within itself and with other churches to the extent this is spiritually and geographically possible.

Jesus used the term *church* in the universal sense by affirming that He will build His church on those who confess Him as Peter did (Matthew 16:18). He also used the term in the local sense, emphasizing the need to exercise discipline so that what is bound on earth is also bound in heaven, and what is loosed on earth is also loosed in heaven (Matthew 18:15–20). In this sense Paul admonished the Corinthian church concerning a brother involved in gross sin: "When you are assembled in the name of our Lord Jesus and I am with you in spirit, and the power of our Lord Jesus is present, hand this man over to Satan, so that his sinful nature may be destroyed and his spirit saved on the day of the Lord" (1 Corinthians 5:4–5).

Were this sin to be left undisciplined, the church at Corinth would be greatly corrupted. And a corrupt church would have a weak witness in the community and around the world.

Christ is not divided (Ephesians 4:4). Therefore the church, as Christ's body, is a unity. Yet God has also planned great diversity in the unity of the members. Although the church is one body, the members are called with differing functions and contributions. The humblest member is as necessary as the noblest; neither can be spared without impairment (1 Corinthians 12:12). The differences are for the common good and every authentic member represents the others. If the body is to be healthy, all members must function for the good of the whole under the leadership of the Head, Christ Jesus.

God has given each member of the body one or more spiritual gifts to energize the church's ministry. A spiritual gift is anointed and positioned within the body by the Spirit of Christ. These differing gifts are for the efficiency and unity of the whole. The members are called to minister the gifts of the Spirit in service to the church and to the world (1 Corinthians 12:5).

The Lord Christ integrates and orchestrates the members of the body for greatest effectiveness. Through unity of faith and service the body is built up and becomes mature (Ephesians 4:13). Maturity and effectiveness to extend the kingdom go hand in hand, and the cycle continues as new converts are added and discipled.

This unifying work of Christ deepens maturity and strengthens the whole body. In the New Testament gifts and sacrifices always point toward worshipful service (see Romans 12:1–2). Worshipful service is comprised of prayer, praise and good deeds expressed through the grace Christ provides. Thereby God is worshiped and glorified and the church deepens in its maturity.

The Temple of the Holy Spirit

In Old Testament times, the temple and the tabernacle that preceded it were the places where God chose to dwell in the midst of Israel. The temple was to be a house of prayer for all nations (Isaiah 56:7; Mark 11:17). It set forth God's excellence as a witness to the nations; it called for people to praise God. In the Psalms God's glory is celebrated in Mount Zion.

Paul in his letters emphatically presents the church as the realization of the Messianic temple (see 2 Corinthians 6:16–7:1; Ephesians 2:19–22). As in Israel of old (Exodus 19:5–6), so also in the New Israel, the members of God's kingdom and of the church are priests (1 Peter 2:9). Although the church, unlike Israel, is not a nation, the church embraces the called-out of all nations to represent a spiritual "nation" that will be manifested when earth and heaven are reconciled at Christ's return.

The temple of the old covenant stood atop Mount Zion in Jerusalem, its magnificence highly visible. As a spiritual center for God's people, it exercised a strong influence. The church, the temple's equivalent representing Christ's kingdom, reflects the splendor of Christ through His people in worshipful service. Its glory does not depend on magnificent buildings, but neither does it disparage beauty in the architecture of its meeting places.

"The church of God which is at Corinth" (1 Corinthians 1:1, KJV) is a typical New Testament expression. Literally it reads, "The congregation as it is in Corinth." Congregations are real people who gather in a local place with regular commitment. These people are visibly identifiable and spiritually unified; never does the New Testament address the "invisible church."[3]

Christ's enthronement in the heavenlies made possible the outpouring of the Holy Spirit (John 7:39) and the promise of a worldwide witness (Acts 1:8). "I have given them the glory that you gave me" (John 17:22), was Jesus' prophetic prayer anticipating Pentecost and the New Testament church. Just as the pillar of cloud by day and fire by night guided Israel through the desert, settling as the Shekinah over the tabernacle directly above the mercy seat whenever Israel encamped, so Christ has determined to put His glory upon His church. The same glory was evident when the 120 were gathered on the day of Pentecost.

"They saw what seemed to be tongues of fire that separated and came to rest on each of them" (Acts 2:3).

The power and authority Jesus established on earth through His incarnate life and atoning death made possible the church's union with Him and empowerment by Him. Our union with Christ—a corporate union represented by the pillar of fire upon the 120 at Pentecost—continues the Old Testament imagery; the church is indeed called a temple of the Holy Spirit (see 2 Corinthians 6:16). The tongues of fire that rested on each one express the personalizing of the Spirit's gifts and graces, energizing the church to fulfill its mission.

The Household of Faith

Christians born into God's family represent the household of faith in their special relationship to Christ and to each other (Ephesians 2:19). As opportunity presents itself, believers are to do good to all people, but especially to those who belong to the family of believers (Galatians 6:10). Having the same Father, believers are brothers and sisters in Christ (James 2:15). Faith in God and confidence in each other give comfort, sustenance and strength for service. Love for each other, self-control and hospitality should characterize the church (1 Peter 4:7–9).

The church as the household of faith is bonded by truth and conviction: "They devoted themselves to the apostles' teaching and to the fellowship, to the breaking of bread and to prayer" (Acts 2:42). In a society today where everything is subjective and relative, the church has a firm commitment to truth. Teaching and training are inherently family functions, and in His Great Commission Jesus prescribed these for His church. In a family household immaturity demands growth; in normal development, transformation is expected. So in the household of God, as believers reflect Christ they are changed "from glory to glory" (2 Corinthians 3:18), destined ultimately to be conformed to the image of Christ (Romans 8:29).

The Church Is a Work Force in a Field

The church does not exist solely for itself but for those who live in its vicinity. The New Testament church is "the church of God in Corinth"—or Ephesus, or Colossae—a specific geographic place. It is God's embassy to a particular community. Although it has members and pastoral leaders whose ministries differ, the church is in a field from which fruitful results are anticipated (1 Corinthians 3:5–9). The congregation that believes and lives the gospel makes that gospel credible and applicable to the larger community. Believers who in their neighborhoods and work places shine as lights in the world best represent the gospel of Jesus Christ.

The vitality of such witness, however, is maintained in the place where God is worshiped, where the prophetic Word is preached, where a support system of teaching and training is in place, where the comfort and strength of fellowship is sustained. This is the way the church is authorized to represent the kingdom of God in a particular locale.

Additionally, the church is to consider the remote corners of earth its parish through missionary service in fields where God's sovereign glory has not yet been announced (Psalm 67:1–2, Luke 24:46–48).

Paul prayed that the Colossian believers "might live a life worthy of the Lord," "bearing fruit in every good work" (Colossians 1:10). Israel was likened to a vineyard "on a fertile hillside" (Isaiah 5:1). To His disciples Jesus said, "I am the vine; you are the branches. If a man remains in me and I in him, he will bear much fruit; apart from me you can do nothing. If anyone does not remain in me, he is like a branch that is thrown away and withers" (John 15:5–6). The church represents a field from which fruit is expected. The fruit is not optional. An unfruitful branch is "thrown away and withers" (15:6); to remain in Christ is by implication to be fruitful.

The church is a place where word is put to deed. Believers are to encourage one another (Hebrews 10:25), be kind to each other (1 Thessalonians 4:15), pray for each other (James 5:16) and serve one another (Galatians 5:13). They also are to give themselves "fully to the work of the Lord" because their "labor in the Lord is not in vain" (1 Corinthians 15:58). We reap what we sow (Galatians 6:7); every believer will appear before the judgment seat of Christ to "receive what is due him for the things done while in the body, whether good or bad" (2 Corinthians 5:10). James reminds his readers that faith unaccompanied by action is dead (James 2:17).

The field where the church works has its own peculiar soil. Fields are not uniformly fertile. But every church and each believer will be rewarded for their faithfulness (1 Corinthians 4:2). The cultivation and sowing of the field under God's direction and blessing will produce a harvest.

The Church Is an Investment Enterprise

There is an entrepreneurial dimension to the church. Its organization, management and assumption of risk demands industrious creativity and alertness to opportunity, bathed in prayer. Jesus described His kingdom enterprise in the graphic parable of a traveling master who, before his departure "puts his servants in charge, each with his assigned task" (Mark 13:34). The picture is one of great trust on the part of the absent master. Although he has made individual assignments to each servant, the service of each represents the interests of the whole enterprise.

Commentators suggest the parable in Mark is an abbreviated version of Matthew's story of the talents (Matthew 25:14–30) and Luke's story of the pounds (Luke 19:12–27). If so, the industry with which the servants do their trading strongly implies an entrepreneurial spirit.

Neither the master's instructions nor the supervising watchman inhibit freedom and spontaneity.

Peter writes, "You also, like living stones, are being built into a spiritual house to be a holy priesthood, offering spiritual sacrifices acceptable to God through Jesus Christ" (1 Peter 2:5). The church is people whose purpose is to be a priesthood—intermediaries whose interest is to serve the Lord by serving others. In Jesus' Mark 13:34 parable, the watchman is like a shepherd or overseer whose responsibility is to realize results from the servants whose work is to honor the master until he returns. So in the church. The whole church is called to be a royal priesthood and every member a priest, but for utmost effectiveness there must be overseers—watchmen—who guide, sustain and nourish the priestly work of the church as a whole. These pastor-overseers are like brokers who by their service to Christ and the church make for peak effectiveness.

Such watchmen are needed. The author of the Hebrews letter exhorts unreliable Judaic Christians in these words:

> *Through Jesus, therefore, let us continually offer to God a sacrifice of praise—the fruit of lips that confess his name. And do not forget to do good and to share with others, for with such sacrifices God is pleased.*
>
> *Obey your leaders and submit to their authority. They keep watch over you as men who must give an account. Obey them so that their work will be a joy, not a burden, for that would be of no advantage to you.*
> (Hebrews 13:15–17)

In His parable told by Mark, Jesus added this further admonition: "Therefore keep watch because you do not know when the owner of the house will come back—whether in the evening, or at midnight, or when the rooster crows, or at dawn. If he comes suddenly, do not let him find you sleeping. What I say to you, I say to everyone: 'Watch' " (Mark 13:35–37). To do business until

Jesus comes is no mere routine. It is a challenge for all His servants to be at their best.

The church is both a place of investment and a recruiting agency. The entrepreneurial servant is never casual about the church. Neither does he or she invest time, spiritual gifts and money capriciously. The wise servant becomes a "living stone" (1 Peter 2:5), positioned by divine design and directed to an assigned task from the Master Himself.

The Church Is the Bride of Christ

Scripture uses marriage to illustrate the relationship of God with Israel (Isaiah 49:18; Jeremiah 2:32; Hosea 2:19–20) and the relationship of Christ with His church (Ephesians 5:25; Revelation 19:7–8). The gospels frequently present Christ as a bridegroom (see Matthew 9:15; 25:1–12; Mark 2:19; Luke 5:34; John 3:29). The church's submission to Christ is analogous to the wife's submission to her husband (Ephesians 5:22–24). Both church and wife are to be made holy and radiant (5:25–27). The analogy simultaneously sets forth the love of God and the holiness of God. Love and holiness are God's most sacred blessings to the church.

Because marriage is declared in public ceremony, so-called secret believers, like secret marriages, are aberrations of God's purpose. As a city on a hill cannot be hidden (Matthew 5:14), so the church is a bride observed by a watching world. In her service for Christ this bride is to be a bold witness to the risen Christ in her values, her ethics and the depth of her love.

At the same time, the church's witness is never a ministry in isolation. Only through the nurture of union with Christ does the church's witness become ongoing and effective. A theology of witness without a theology of nurture is inimical to the New Testament. Only in a relationship of nurture is a clear witness possible.

Just as the family worldwide is the foundational unit of society, so the church family is the fundamental unit of

God's kingdom. We tend to understand the Great Commission too narrowly and too legalistically—as a bare command. We fail to realize that Christ's husbandry, presence, cleansing, enabling and sufficiency are central to the church's effectiveness (Matthew 28:20). The vastness of God's love and His plan for the world ought to inspire the church to exist in union with Christ.

As the unique possession of God, a people indwelt by Him, the church exists to make known to all nations His glory and power through the gospel. His people are destined for the throne of the universe as coheirs with Christ. They are being prepared for this ministry even now. The Holy Spirit has come to bring about maturity in the church corporately and individually so that Christ may be glorified fully in His dominion.

The Bride Vows to Be Faithful

Just as God has ordained monogamy in marriage, He has ordained monogamy for believers in union with Christ. As the relationship of God with His people rests upon His character and His faithfulness to a declared covenant, so the character of God's people rests upon their faithfulness to God and His Word.

In all of Scripture—Law, History, Psalms, Prophets, Gospels, Letters, Apocalypse—the wonder of faithfulness and the tragedy of unfaithfulness are recurring themes played out against the metaphor of marriage. The image culminates strikingly in Revelation as God says, "Come, I will show you the bride, the wife of the Lamb." And the Bible's final invitation is couched in the same imagery: "The Spirit and the bride say, 'Come!' And let him who hears say, 'Come!' Whoever is thirsty, let him come; and whoever wishes, let him take the free gift of the water of life" (Revelation 22:17).

W. C. Stevens in *Revelation: The Crown-Jewel of Biblical Prophecy*,[4] observes:

At every point in the book the view presented of Jesus Himself is from the standpoint of the presence and interest of His church. It follows, as we shall see, that nowhere is such a comprehensive revelation of the church of Jesus Christ to be found as in the book of Revelation. In almost a paramount sense the book may be taken as Christ's own final full revelation of His precious and glorious church.[5]

In final judgment God depicts the apostate church as a woman in fine array who holds

> . . . *a golden cup in her hand, filled with abominable things and the filth of her adulteries. This title was written on her forehead:*
> MYSTERY
> BABYLON THE GREAT
> THE MOTHER OF PROSTITUTES
> AND OF THE ABOMINATIONS OF THE EARTH.
> (Revelation 17:4–5)

Her direct attempt to deify man rather than Christ represents universal false religion. Revelation 18 dramatically describes the judgment and fall of this "mother of prostitutes."

In bold contrast we see the marriage supper of the Lamb in great victory:

> *"Hallelujah!*
>   *For our Lord God Almighty reigns.*
> *Let us rejoice and be glad*
>   *and give him glory!*
> *For the wedding of the Lamb has come,*
>   *and his bride has made herself ready.*
> *Fine linen, bright and clean,*
>   *was given her to wear."*
>
> (Revelation 19:6–7)

The Church Is Preparation for the Kingdom

As Christ's bride, the church is destined to inherit Christ's kingdom (Matthew 25:34). At present this kingdom is a mystery, but it will be manifest at Christ's return to earth. In His incarnation Jesus represented Himself as the kingdom's Messiah. He announced, "The kingdom of God is near" (Mark 12:15). Much of Jesus' public discourse was couched in parables relating to the kingdom, indicative of God's plan not only to redeem God's people but to restore creation.

Paul later would write to the church in Rome saying he considered his present sufferings "not worth comparing with the glory that will be revealed" when Christ liberates the children of God from the bondage of sin inflicted on them by their fallen nature. Even the "creation," Paul says, "waits in eager expectation for the sons of God to be revealed." Indeed, "the whole creation has been groaning as in the pains of childbirth right up to the present time" (Romans 8:18–22).

After Pentecost, as the apostles preached about the kingdom and Christ as King, believers began to meet to worship. Churches were the outgrowth of kingdom preaching (Acts 8:12; 14:21–22; 20:25). The doctrine, discipline and direction of these churches become the main subjects of the Letters because holiness in the church is the best expression of the kingdom of God. Just as the Old Testament saints were to be a holy nation and a kingdom of priests, so New Testament saints were exhorted to holiness and priestly sacrifice (Philippians 4:18; 1 Peter 2:5).

In one of Jesus' post-resurrection appearances, the disciples inquired of Him as to when He would "restore the kingdom to Israel" (Acts 1:6). Jesus answered, "It is not for you to know the times or dates the Father has set by his own authority. But you will receive power when the Holy Spirit comes on you, and you will be my witnesses in Jerusalem, and in all Judea and Samaria, and to the ends of the earth" (1:7). The national kingdom of Israel was no longer to be the focus. Rather, bearing witness to the identity and resurrection of the Messiah became a global mandate through the church.

A Partnership in Kingdom Work

The Old Testament begins with man created and commissioned to fill and subdue the earth and to have dominion over it (Genesis 1:18). God created man in His image. In terms of God's redemptive purpose after the fall, Adam is said to typify Christ (Romans 5:14) and Eve to typify the church (Ephesians 5:31–32). The New Testament begins with the incarnation of Christ, tells of His earthly life, atoning death, glorious resurrection and heavenly ascension. Then it goes on to report the formation of Christ's church. That church, at the restoration of the kingdom, will fill and subdue the earth (see Daniel 2:35).

Paul describes the working of God's mighty strength "when he raised [Christ] from the dead and seated him at his right hand in the heavenly realms, far above all rule and authority, power and dominion" (Ephesians 1:20–21). The apostle amplifies this assertion by adding, "God placed all things under his feet and appointed him to be head over everything for the church, which is his body, the fullness of him who fills everything in every way" (1:22–23). The church is God's master plan to establish His global kingdom. God's kingdom is creation restored by the redemptive ministry of Christ and His church. Jesus said, "This gospel of the kingdom will be preached in the whole world as a testimony to all nations, and then the end will come" (Matthew 24:14).

The end will be the coming of Christ to establish His kingdom. The church will be caught up at Christ's coming to join Him in establishing His kingdom—both a heavenly and an earthly kingdom. Of Christ Paul says, "God was pleased to have all his fullness dwell in him, and through him to reconcile to himself all things,

21

whether things on earth or things in heaven, by making peace through his blood, shed on the cross" (Colossians 1:19–20).

The Church: The New Jerusalem

Finally, the church in her glorified state is described as the new Jerusalem "coming down from God out of heaven, prepared as a bride adorned for her husband" (Revelation 19:1). Stevens comments:

> The term *city* is the highest conception of an habitation. Its structure is the most elaborate, its organization the most developed, its activities the most composite, its privileges the most favored. "City of God" is, then, the supreme conception and description of God's residence in the whole glorified church.[6]

The fact that this city comes out of heaven to be a tabernacle among men on earth speaks volumes concerning God's interest in His original creation. Stevens points out:

> Here surely is a vital and personal relationship between Jesus Christ and the mundane creation, which warrants, as it also elucidates His own description of it, "I am its Alpha and its Omega, its Origin and its Finish." And when creation fell, it was a personal matter to Him, and creation's redemption lay with Him, yea, in Him: "For it pleased the Father that, . . . having made peace through the blood of his cross, by him to reconcile all things unto himself; by him, . . . whether they be things in earth, or things in heaven" (Colossians 1:19–20).[7]

The church is a multifaceted diamond, exclusively the property of Jesus Christ, the Light of the world and the Light of life (John 8:12). Its symmetry, its depth and its reflective quality declare the praises of the Owner, who has called the church "out of darkness into his wonderful light" (1 Peter 2:9). As this multifaceted church reflects the true Light, people are drawn to Christ Jesus (John 12:32).

This diamond—the church—cut by the Holy Spirit and mounted in its full biblical context, needs to be seen in its entirety. If projected too rigidly—as, perhaps, a mighty army going forth to war, or as a fundamentalist fortress poised to defend the truth, or as a dress of holiness designed for self-admiration—it loses its attractiveness.

In the succeeding chapters, we want to examine some of the many facets of this priceless jewel.

Endnotes

[1] A.B. Simpson, *Present Truths or the Supernatural* (Harrisburg, PA, n.d.), p. 49.

[2] Ibid., p. 46.

[3] The idea of the *invisible church* was spawned by Reformed theologians in the 16th century, intending to distinguish the elect from the mixed body in the visible church who lived in mere outward profession. This, however, was a result of territorial churches. The Reformers did not intend to negate the importance of the visible church but to affirm the need for the visible church which they described as a shell that nurtured the kernel. But territorial churches have no biblical justification, nor do the Scriptures ever speak of invisible churches.

[4] Harrisburg, PA: Christian Publications, 1928. W.C. Stevens' scholarly work may still be the best and most comprehensive treatment of the book of Revelation.

[5] Stevens, Ibid., p. 99.

[6] Ibid., pp. 388–389.

[7] Ibid., p. 390.

The Glory of Christ
in His Church

2

The Church in History

*I*n our contemporary world, the church's biblical ideals seem out of reach. Yet the church today stands in historical succession to an apostolic faith. Both the past and the present testify to the church's significance in God's redemptive purpose. To be sure, the church has had many dark chapters. Frequently it has fallen far short of its high calling. But God's past interventions, Jesus' present intercession and the Bible's great promises concerning the future leave no room for pessimism or disbelief.

The gap between the historical fact and the idealism which theology sets before us strongly suggests that we take neither history nor theology very seriously. The influence of dispensationalism on American evangelicalism early in the 20th century is a significant case in point.

Dispensationalists depict the "church age" as a parenthetical interlude in God's universal plan of redemption. This church age began at Pentecost and will conclude with the rapture at Christ's return. Consequently, the kingdom Christ announced during His earthly ministry—a kingdom dispensationalists see as strictly Jewish—was and will be postponed until after the rapture and time of tribulation. The spiritual body of the redeemed has no necessary visible expression because it is a spiritual mystery. According to classical dispensationalism, believers now live in the age of the Spirit and are members of an invisible church because outward physical churches misrepresent the true church.

As a result of dispensational thinking, American evangelical theology of the church became more abstract than real. It tended to ignore the church's historical significance.

Accurate history and biblical theology are both essential. Any attempt to idealize the church as something outside of historical reality is unscriptural. The church is not a spiritual phantom. Even as the historical life and work of Jesus, set forth in the Bible, identifies His glorious intercessory work today, so our view of the historical church in the light of theology shapes our concept of the present-day church and its mission.

The New Testament views the church as existing in specific locales, as having corporate personalities and particular profiles. The churches identified in Revelation 2 and 3 were encouraged with commendations and judged with failings. To them the prophetic Word had an urgent application. Similarly, Paul's letters address contemporary churches and call for corporate accountability and responsibility in real life situations about which he was deeply concerned.

The history of the church with its triumphs and mistakes manifests both the mercy of God and the faithful teaching ministry of the Holy Spirit. This background of both history and theology cannot be dismissed. It authenticates the church's present reason for existence. It informs us how we have come to be where we are. At the same time, theology shows us what God desires us to be and how we may get there. Both are essential. The concepts of the visible and invisible cannot be divorced. The true visible church on earth is to be filled with members of the redeemed invisible church.

However faulty the church's expression of Christ has been, the New Testament church has existed since Pentecost. It has proclaimed Christ and His gospel. As both a spiritual and physical body, it is always in process, neither fixed nor frozen. Its principal calling is to represent Christ in His fullness and to be God's chosen instrument to meet the needs of the world.

The Christian and Missionary Alliance

The local church's relationship to the universal church is key. "The local congregation," as Leslie Newbigin astutely observes, "is not a branch of the universal church, but it is the place where the universal church is made visible."[1] In fact, without the local churches there would be no fellowship and no comprehension "with all the saints" of the width, length, height and depth of Christ's love (Ephesians 3:18). Neither as individual members nor as local churches dare we isolate ourselves from the universal expression of the church. Writes A.B. Simpson:

> Not singly can we grasp this mighty vision. It is only when we enter into the perfect fellowship of the body of Christ that we can know the fullness of our great salvation. . . . The whole progression of redemption is toward one grand consummation, the reconciling and uniting of all in one and the crystallizing of God's wisdom, power and love in the story of creation and redemption into a single ideal, the paragon of the universe, the glory of the ages to come, the new Jerusalem, the Bride of the Lamb, the Church of Jesus Christ.[2]

Simpson recognized the believer's necessary quest for "the perfect fellowship of the body of Christ" in order to "know the fullness of our great salvation." He realized the early Alliance "branches," as initially organized, were mere auxiliaries to local churches. The historical identity and integrity of the church, however, involves a responsibility and an accountability that cannot be fulfilled by parachurch organizations. They compromise biblical theology and violate the unity that glorifies Christ. This was the dilemma Simpson and the Alliance struggled with as the branch-type of organization became increasingly inadequate for its intended purpose.

Some have concluded that the imperfections evident in all churches necessitate a "spiritual" or mystical church without membership or organization. Others reply to the problem with independent churches or exclusive denominations. But none of these corresponds to the true biblical ideal.

Relating the doctrine of the church to the historical legacy of The Christian and Missionary Alliance is a challenge. Those acquainted with Alliance history know that it originally was a transdenominational missionary society. In 1899 the founder, Simpson, spoke of the Alliance in these words:

> Let us never forget the special calling of our Alliance work. It is not to form a new religious denomination, it is not to duplicate a work already done. It is not to advocate any special system of theology. It is not to glorify any man or men. It is first to lift up Jesus in His fullness, . . . to encourage and incite the people of God to do the neglected work of our age and time among the unchurched classes at home and the perishing heathen abroad.[3]

These words, valid for their age and time, highlight the change that has overtaken The Christian and Missionary Alliance in a century. In organization, Simpson patterned the Alliance after the Evangelical Alliance based in London and begun in 1846. The Evangelical Alliance was formed to bridge fellowship and cooperation among denominations. Its purpose was to demonstrate the unity of the church in foreign missionary efforts and to avoid competition. The same objectives motivated Simpson and his associates, with particular focus on the need for spiritual dynamic to accomplish the world's evangelization, a mission the church for too long had neglected.

From an original structure of "branches," almost a century of identity struggle ensued. Only after extensive reorganization in 1974 was The Christian and Missionary Alliance considered officially a church and a denomination. The torturous route by which the corporate Alliance came to confess its church-ness invites an interesting analysis that nostalgia may not easily welcome. Our immediate purpose, however, is to discover a credible integration of the Alliance with church theology so as to affirm its particular nature and function in the calling entrusted to it.

Present Confusion Regarding the Church

A contemporary theologian observes that "at no point in the history of Christian thought has the doctrine of the church received the direct and complete attention other doctrines have received."[4] According to scholarly analysts, not until the 1950s did either Protestant or Catholic theologians seriously cultivate the doctrine of the church. Perhaps they took the church for granted, not recognizing that its empirical identity was to reflect a divinely revealed design, failing to understand that biblical authority gave it its corporate purpose and mission. It is easy to replace biblical norms by rationalized expediencies or by generalized "spiritualities" that are uncritically accepted. A new, biblical positioning of today's church in the world is overdue.

Evangelicals are often hard pressed to explain why the church exists, to delineate the roles of pastor, elder, deacon, or to define the purpose of worship. How do preaching and teaching differ? What is the relationship between church membership, baptism and communion? Between local evangelism and missions? Glossed interpretations and unexamined ambiguities so permeate the evangelical mind-set that the words of Jesus—"Where two or three come together in my name, there am I with them" (Matthew 18:20)—are understood to apply to the church in any pragmatic ad hoc religious effort. As biblical norms are neglected, confusion increases.

The lack of form and content in our understanding of the contemporary church is not just a significant theological problem. It is also a serious functional problem. Parachurch movements (campus evangelism, prison work, world relief, gospel radio, missionary aviation), ministering transdenominationally or alongside local churches, have contributed immeasurably to the church's impact. But the evangelical landscape is littered with a proliferation of such independent enterprises. These operations often evidence little or no accountability to the church, not in doctrine, not in discipline, not in finances. They serve as substitutes for the church. The so-called "electronic church," in some cases, not only has bilked church members of millions of dollars with scandalous results, but has seriously undermined the scriptural image of the church.[5]

If biblical precepts and principles do not govern the church, its expression of the gospel will be uncertain. Increasingly, the church will fall short of meeting the spiritual needs of its members and of accomplishing what the Great Commission includes. If its form and content are not based on divine revelation, the church, however successful in modern dress, inevitably will lose divine authority and power. The current belief that God dynamically relates to the world through varied agencies and institutions, all of them covered by the word *church*, is a misconception. If the church's credibility is to undergird its mission, believers must gain a new understanding of it.

The Biblical Perspective

To understand the church, we need a full biblical perspective. Often we see only what we want the Bible to say, even though we confess it to be our guide for faith and practice. We must study the Bible with honest, open eyes and searching hearts. In this case, the church deserves no less.

Sometimes we say the church was born on the day of Pentecost, implying that it has little continuity with the Old Testament. This is contrary to what the Scriptures teach. Paul told the Gentile Ephesians, who formerly were "separate from Christ, excluded from citizenship in Israel and foreigners to the covenants of the promise" that they were "no longer foreigners and aliens, but fellow citizens with God's people and members of God's household, built on the foundation of the apostles and prophets, with Christ Jesus himself as the chief cornerstone" (Ephesians 2:12, 19–20).

The right of membership within the church initially belonged to Israel, not to the Gentiles. But what was only alluded to in the Old Testament and not fully understood by believers of that era is now in this Christian age being revealed in its deepest spiritual meaning and truth.

The church is a continuity. Its roots are deep in the pre-Christian eras. To fail to see this results in a superficial understanding of the church's full nature and purpose. Our myopia in turn impacts our sense of membership in God's household.

The church needs to recognize that its foundation rests both on the apostles of the New Testament and the prophets of the Old, Jesus Christ being the Cornerstone. Peter expresses the relevancy of this continuity when he paraphrases Exodus 19:6 for God's New Testament people: "You also, like living stones, are being built into a spiritual house to be a holy priesthood, offering spiritual sacrifices acceptable to God through Jesus Christ" (1 Peter 2:5).

Israel was a spiritual house formed by God in which His people were to worship and serve Him acceptably. Isaiah declares:

> *"But you, O Israel, my servant,*
> *Jacob, whom I have chosen,*
> *you descendants of Abraham my friend,*
> *I took you from the ends of the earth,*
> *from its farthest corners I called you.*
> *I said, 'You are my servant':*
> *I have chosen you and have not rejected you."*
> (Isaiah 41:8–9)

Under the Old Covenant, Israel was a chosen servant for God's rule over the universe. With the coming of Christ, however, the kingdom had a more fully revealed reference who would unite Jew and Gentile into a new servanthood with dynamic news. "The time has come," Jesus said. "The kingdom of God is near. Repent and believe the good news!" Paul, writing under divine inspiration, says, "In [Christ] the whole building is joined together and rises to become a holy temple in the Lord. And in him you too are being built together [Jew and Gentile] to become a dwelling in which God lives by his Spirit" (Ephesians 2:21–22).

"The whole building" which joins the New Covenant people of God and the faithful saints of the Old Covenant is to become a holy temple analogous to Mount Zion and the temple in ancient Israel. Today, in whatever locality God's people are built together (John 4:21–24), they are a habitation for God's Spirit and participants in His universal purpose here and now.

Each new church must see itself in that continuity. Each has a definite identity, solidity, dignity, meaning and stature as it represents Christ and His enthronement (Ephesians 1:19–23). This is a pattern for all people of God who are now being built together as a part of His church.

The Old Testament Faithful Are a Part

God gave Israel a meticulous pattern for the tabernacle. He told Moses, "Make this tabernacle and all its furnishings exactly like the pattern I will show you" (Exodus 25:9). Regarding the seven meticulously fashioned lamps for the lampstand, God used similar words: "See that you make them according to the pattern shown you on the mountain." (25:40). The garments for the priests, the altars, the laver, the anointing oil and fragrant incense were all to be made exactly as God commanded (Exodus 31:11).

Centuries later God gave Ezekiel a prophetic vision of a new temple. Significantly, it resembled the original tabernacle and temple. But there were changes, too, and these carried important implications for the future. God told Ezekiel:

> *Son of man, describe the temple to the people of Israel, that they may be ashamed of their sins. Let them consider the plan, and if they are ashamed of all they have done, make known to them the design of the temple—its arrangement, its exits and entrances—its whole design and all its regulations and laws. Write these down before them so that they may be faithful to its design and follow all its regulations.*

> (Ezekiel 43:10–11)

To Simpson, the prophetic picture God gave Ezekiel had important implications for the New Testament church— "that great house of God's building which consists of ransomed souls and is built on the foundation of Jesus Christ." Simpson writes:

> This spiritual house has a divine pattern. Just as the tabernacle of old was to be constructed strictly according to the pattern that was shown to Moses on the Mount, so the church of Christ has a divine plan. It

behooves us to construct it accordingly in every particular. Failure to do so has been the cause of the apostasies, declensions and mistakes of the past centuries. Failure to do so is the reason so much of our world still lies in darkness, crying out to God against the unfaithfulness of God's people.[6]

That Simpson should think the Ezekiel prophecy demanded a particular form for the New Testament church is perhaps difficult to accept. After all, the organization Simpson founded made no pretense at the time of being a church. But Simpson did identify the New York Gospel Tabernacle, begun in 1881, as a New Testament church. Its message and mission, in Simpson's mind, created a demand for a branch agency to serve existing churches. Simpson felt existing churches needed to reconstitute certain missing elements, particularly their world mission and the message of an all-sufficient Christ. For this task the Alliance ostensibly had been raised up. As evangelical churches embraced the message of an all-sufficient Christ and committed themselves to His Great Commission, Simpson believed that other necessary adjustments would follow.

In the mind of Simpson, the exacting design of the Mosaic tabernacle and Ezekiel's prophetic temple were forerunners of the New Testament church spiritually and physically.

The Preparatory Nature of the Old

To begin with, the Scriptures teach that a cosmic disclosure of God's self-revelation was inherent in creation (Romans 1:20). As we already have noted, Adam and Eve were the crown of God's creative work and reflected His image. They were to fill and subdue the earth as God's viceregents. Adam and Eve, however, fatally distorted God's image when they succumbed to Satan's temptation. The damage required divine intervention if humanity was to know God's way of salvation and serve God as He intended.

Immediately after man's fall, God promised that Eve's offspring would bruise Satan's head (Genesis 3:15). Previous to the Mosaic law, a family priesthood observed sacrifices in anticipation of the prophetic promise given to Adam and Eve. These sacrifices affirmed faith in God regarding a savior-offspring of Eve. Among the families of earth, a distinction developed between the righteous who served God and looked for His promise and those who ignored God.

God in His inscrutable wisdom, began to prepare a particular family for the fulfillment of the redemptive promise He initially had made. This faithful family began with Abraham, whose descendants became a nation under Moses.

To Moses God gave the 10 commandments. He put them within the context of ceremonial regulations which were to be a tutor to lead people to Christ (Galatians 3:24). "[The law] was added," writes Paul, "because of transgressions until the Seed to whom the promise referred had come" (3:19). The object of the ceremonial law was to lead the faithful to recognize God's purpose of salvation in the coming Messiah.

Believers who lived during the Old Covenant era expressed faith in God by observing the statutes and laws God gave to Moses. Their obedience to these laws did not save them. They were saved by faith in what these laws symbolized and promised as divine revelation from a gracious and merciful God. But Israel perverted the intent of the ceremonial law and attributed self-righteousness to its outward observance apart from God's mercy and grace. As self-sufficient arrogance increased, they came to believe that religious performance accumulated for them merit and a more privileged position.

Although Israel was explicitly warned about this danger (see Deuteronomy 9:4–6), increasingly the people began to assume credit for their works. Israel's perverted disposition toward God characterized the nation's lifestyle and distorted its testimony to surrounding peoples. Their pride and self-sufficiency led other nations to believe Israel's God was a tribal or national deity such as other nations had. God's transcendent identity and His divine purpose were lost first to Israel and then to the world. Likewise, the symbolism of the priesthood, the sacrifices, the temple and the various ordinances—all representing the meaning of Messiah—faded into perfunctory and impractical insignificance.

The Prophets Went Unheeded

God raised up prophets to confront Israel with its sin. These prophets gave true interpretation and application to the law. As individual Israelites received the message of the prophets, they became a saved remnant. Meanwhile, the nation as a whole became in its perverted blindness twice as sinful as the heathen nations who had no knowledge of the truth (Ezekiel 16:51–52).

The divinely inspired words of the prophets were recorded on parchment for all to read. Thus all who neglected the truth, both in Israel and among the Gentiles, stood judged before God. The prophets' words were not sporadic correctives but a faithful witness to truth new and old—a documented record of God's faithfulness to His revealed promises and His universal intentions.

But what was God's desire for Abraham's seed? What blessing did He intend for Israel? Was it merely an unearned position of privilege among the nations? No, certainly not. To Abraham God gave the promise: "All peoples on earth / will be blessed through you" (Genesis 12:3). The Spirit of divine prophecy explicitly revealed that history was moving toward a fuller revelation for God's people. He intended for them to know Him and to serve Him.

God is sovereignly masterminding a divine progression toward a glorious goal. The world as we know it will conclude in a universal kingdom for those who believe in and follow the Lord. The faithful of the Old Covenant, described in Hebrews 11, "admitted that they were aliens and strangers on earth . . . longing for a better country—a heavenly one." The writer adds: "Therefore God is not ashamed to be called their God" (Hebrews 11:13, 16).

The Israelites had opportunity to experience God for their own blessing by receiving His mercy and serving Him in the wholeness of God's universal intention. This would have preserved them from a distorted self-image. God decreed that Israel was to be a priesthood to the surrounding nations (Exodus 19:5–6). For this assignment Israel needed the guidance and protection of the ceremonial law and the continuous intervention of God's prophets to interpret God's will. Although God faithfully sent His prophets to guide the nation and personally intervened regularly in Israel's behalf, only a remnant believed and followed in obedience.

God's Universal Purposes for Israel

Israel failed to follow through in its God-given priestly mission to the nations. Israel failed as well in its national and cosmic roles. When people corporately relate to the Lord, they embrace His purposes, they become a part of His faithful seed. When God calls individuals, they are included in a corporate call.

Abraham was called to be the father of a great people through whom the nations of earth were to be blessed. The call of the nation Israel was to a "peoplehood." When Jacob shrank from going to Egypt, God reassured him: "Do not be afraid to go down to Egypt, for I will make you into a great nation there" (Genesis 46:3).

God's calling of Noah, Abraham, Jacob, Joseph and Moses played pivotal roles in the formation of a people for God. Mankind's vertical relationship to God always results in a horizontal relationship of a peoplehood. A teacher of the law once asked Jesus what the most important commandment was. Jesus answered: " 'Hear, O Israel, the Lord our God, the Lord is one. Love the Lord your

God with all your heart and with all your soul and with all your mind and with all your strength.' The second is this: 'Love your neighbor as yourself.' There is no commandment greater than these" (Mark 12:29–31).

The vertical, spiritual relationship with God also includes the horizontal, physical relationship with one's neighbor. The latter is proof of the former and results in a peoplehood of oneness in God. Both are the result of God's unity.

Peoplehood is not optional. It is the business of God, and it is always at the heart of God's call. He calls us to a responsible society regarding truth and mission. God's call is never for mere self-containment or individual independence. We are to live for the sake of others, being mindful of God's universal intentions. Along with the call to peoplehood is an inherent call to servanthood to fulfill God's purpose. Thus God intends for His image and His universal redemption to be reflected in His people.

When God's peoplehood serves only itself or meets only the needs of its members, it fails in its primary calling. God has called us to serve the world. With this calling to obedience, God makes ample provision for other needs. "Seek first [God's] kingdom and his righteousness," Jesus says, "and all these things will be given to you as well" (Matthew 6:33).

Israel was to be a priesthood of the earth: "Although the whole earth is mine," God said to Israel, "you will be for me a kingdom of priests and a holy nation" (Exodus 19:6; see also Deuteronomy 7:6–8). Blinded by selfishness, Israel defaulted on God's calling. And God moved the prophet Isaiah to predict judgment:

> "Woe to the obstinate children,"
> declares the LORD,
> "to those who carry out plans that are not mine,
> forming an alliance, but not by my Spirit,
> heaping sin upon sin."
>   (Isaiah 30:1)

Divine Judgment, Divine Promise

Israel's alliances with alien countries canceled God's redemptive purpose and plan for the nation. But with the threats of judgment came also grand promises of what God willed to do through His people. These glorious promises rode tandem with the promise of Messiah, pictured as a suffering servant:

> *And now the LORD says—*
> > *he who formed me in the womb to be his servant*
> *to bring Jacob back to him*
> > *to gather Israel to himself,*
> *for I am honored in the eyes of the LORD*
> > *and my God has been my strength—*
> *he says:*
> *"It is too small a thing for you to be my servant*
> > *to restore the tribes of Jacob*
> > *and to bring back those of Israel I have kept.*
> *I will also make you a light for the Gentiles,*
> > *that you may bring my salvation to the ends*
> > > *of the earth. . . .*
> *Kings will see you and rise up,*
> > *princes will see you and bow down,*
> *because of the LORD, who is faithful,*
> > *the Holy One of Israel, who has chosen you."*
> > > > (Isaiah 49:5–6, 7b)

Israel's renewed commitment to God was to be followed by God's highest blessing of salvation to the ends of the earth. This, in turn, would bring honor to Israel: "Princes will see and bow down." And although Israel defaulted and eventually was driven into captivity, the prophecy remained just as exacting and purposeful as Ezekiel's prophecy of the new temple. God's highest glory on earth is seen in His peoplehood. In faithfulness He will perform His Word.

All the revealed promises relating to God's peoplehood fit into the whole of His redemptive plan for creation. No person, no gift, no calling, no position is unimportant. Abraham all his life was a sheepherder. God continues to work out His glorious purpose for creation by calling together a peoplehood of believers from all walks of life.

God's Universal Intention in the Church

Many images in Scripture reflect the glory of Jesus Christ through the church. Peter, who much earlier had interpreted the events of Pentecost to the thousands of Israel who gathered to see the marvel, wrote this to God's elect:

> *You also, like living stones, are being built into a spiritual house to be a holy priesthood, offering spiritual sacrifices acceptable to God through Jesus Christ. For in Scripture it says:*
> *"See, I lay a stone in Zion,*
> *a chosen and precious cornerstone,*
> *and the one who trusts in him*
> *will never be put to shame"*
> (1 Peter 2: 5–6)

Peter's sense of continuity between Israel and the church did not diminish even decades after the New Testament church began on the day of Pentecost and engulfed the Gentile world. Peter affirmed that God's peoplehood was still under divine construction and served as a holy priesthood with spiritual sacrifices in order to fulfill God's universal redemption.

Christ sent the Holy Spirit to produce witnesses of a kingdom anticipated with Christ's coming. And though the disciples anxiously inquired as to its timing, Jesus answered, "It is not for you to know the times or dates the Father has set by his own authority. But you will receive power when the Holy Spirit comes on you; and you will be my witnesses in Jerusalem, and in all Judea and Samaria, and to the ends of the earth" (Acts 1:7–8) The outpouring of the Spirit at Pentecost upon people of at least 14 languages was indicative of God's universal intention for His New Testament peoplehood.

The implications of the images in First Peter 2:5–6, quoted above, again emphasize the continuity of the church with Israel. That continuity, while prophetic in imagery, is practical in function.

The Kingdom Is Fundamental to the Church

As Mark reminds us in the parable of the traveling master that we looked at in chapter 1 (Mark 13:34), every servant is to be alert while doing his important household duties. Each assigned task was with a view to the master's return. It is a message the church needs to hear again and again. The church's Lord is also returning. Each task He has assigned to us is related to His return. The church poorly comprehends this fundamental principle.

Israel's penchant for righteousness based on works and for national exclusiveness evoked our Lord's lament over Jerusalem:

> *"O Jerusalem, Jerusalem, you who kill the prophets and stone those sent to you, how often I have longed to gather your children together, as a hen gathers her chicks under her wings, but you were not willing! Look, your house is left to you desolate."*

(Luke 13:34–35)

But a similar desolation awaits the church that is disobedient to Christ's Great Commission and intent upon its own self-centered interests. Israel failed as a peoplehood. God had nurtured and protected them that they might be a national instrument of His purpose. Their house was left desolate because they failed to respond. Christ's blessing, corporately and individually, is significantly related to the faithful obedience of His "house."

A Roman centurion once requested Jesus to heal his servant. He expressed both his humility and his faith in the

41

authority of Jesus by saying, "Lord, I do not deserve to have you come under my roof. But just say the word, and my servant will be healed." Jesus, astonished, comments, "I tell you the truth, I have not found anyone in Israel with such great faith. I say to you that many will come from the east and the west, and will take their places at the feast with Abraham, Isaac and Jacob in the kingdom of heaven. But the subjects of the kingdom will be thrown outside, into the darkness, where there will be weeping and gnashing of teeth" (Matthew 8:8–12). To have Jesus' authority under the roof of one's house is no casual privilege. Its blessing depends on an obedience of faith that has universal implications.

The contrast Jesus drew between the centurion's faith and that of Israel will be missed by those untrained through the prophetic writings, but it carries bold implications. The Roman centurion was not a part of God's peoplehood, but he recognized Jesus' heavenly authority.

Apart from His death and resurrection, Jesus' messianic ministry was appointed to the house of Israel (Matthew 15:24). The centurion's faith put to shame those who were subjects of the kingdom. The centurion understood authority under Caesar's jurisdiction, but the house of Israel was blind to the authority under Jesus' jurisdiction. The divinely called people who ignore the King's identity and authority are unworthy subjects of the kingdom.

Endnotes

[1] Leslie Newbigin, *Truth to Tell* (Grand Rapids: Wm. B. Eerdmans Publishing Co., 1991), p. 88.

[2] A.B. Simpson, "The Church in the Heavenlies," *The Christian and Missionary Alliance* (May 21, 1898), p. 437.

[3] A.B. Simpson, "The Mission of the Alliance," *The Christian and Missionary Alliance* (November 4, 1899), p. 365.

[4]Millard J. Erickson, *Christian Theology*, Vol. III (Grand Rapids: Baker Book House, 1985), p. 1026.

[5]It is estimated there are 6,500 organizations, Protestant and Catholic, that function alongside the church or independently of it. A scant 15 years ago, more than 50 percent of the graduates of several major seminaries accepted parachurch positions (see Stephen Board, "The Great Evangelical Shift," *Eternity* [June 1979], p. 17). The North American Securities Administration, Inc., 555 New Jersey Avenue, N.W., Suite 750, Washington, D.C., issued a warning letter dated September 1989 regarding the misappropriation of charity funds by those making television appeals.

[6]A.B. Simpson, *Missionary Messages* (Camp Hill, PA: Christian Publications, 1987), pp. 11–12. Simpson's view of definite design for the New Testament church was evident when the Christian Alliance in 1887 was organized with a branch design. Branches were transdenominational auxiliaries of the church. They were led by *superintendents*, not pastors. The ordinances were not observed because it was assumed that all constituents were members of regular churches. Services were scheduled at times not in conflict with the churches of the community.

Frequently overlooked is the fact that Simpson organized the New York Gospel Tabernacle as a regular church. Simpson, 17 years previously, had been ordained as a Presbyterian minister. The Gospel Tabernacle was affiliated with The Christian and Missionary Alliance, but it was not considered an Alliance church as we know it today. The *tabernacle* design initiated in the early 1920s by Paul Rader, second president of The Christian and Missionary Alliance, was explicitly projected as non-church. The Rader tabernacles scarcely resembled the New York Gospel Tabernacle.

3

Preparing a
Missionary Church

*T*o Albert Benjamin Simpson, founder of The Christian and Missionary Alliance, the missionary function of the church in Acts set a pattern for a task yet to be concluded. Simpson saw in Acts seven lessons:[1]

1. Evangelizing the world is the supreme business of the church. The promise of the Holy Spirit was related to worldwide evangelization. The constituency that received the Pentecostal blessing represented all tribes and tongues. The gift of tongues given at Pentecost was symbolic of the translation of the gospel into every human lan-

guage. The one supreme thought of heaven and the chief business of the church on earth are thus shown to be the Master's last command: "Make disciples of all nations," "Go into all the world and preach the good news to all creation" (Matthew 28:19; Mark 16:15).

2. A prepared home base is foundational for effective missionary work. Antioch had to be established before Macedonia could be evangelized. Foreign missions is not the peculiar enterprise of certain individuals who may be moved by an impulse of altruism or toward social service. Missions should be the organized and united effort of the entire church.

3. A spirit of unselfishness and sacrifice must characterize the home church. This is a repeated lesson in the apostolic story. Samaria must be willing to give up Philip to the desert. Antioch must surrender two of its pastor-leaders, Barnabas and Saul, for the greater work among the Gentiles.

4. The church must have an aggressive missionary polity. In the first century, the world's political epicenter was moving westward into Europe. The church kept in step with God's providence and went to Europe, too. Today it is the Pacific Rim, the New East that meets the New West. We should be wise to understand the meaning of our times and true to the call of our "Macedonia."

5. The church in Antioch was a witnessing church, not an institutional church settling down to build permanent organizations and an earthly kingdom. James paints a striking picture: God is visiting the Gentile nations to take out of them a people for His name. Missions is an "out" movement, a swift evangel, an angel in the midst of heaven flying with winged swiftness to announce the everlasting gospel to all mankind.

6. Missions is a premillennial movement. Its outlook is not a here-and-now millennium. Rather, "After this I will return / and rebuild David's fallen tent. / Its ruins I will rebuild, / and I will restore it, / that the remnant of men

may seek the Lord, / and all the Gentiles who bear my name" (Acts 15:16–17).

7. The triune God—the leadership of the Holy Spirit, the presence of the ascended Lord, the constant providence of God the Father—these are written in capital letters in the story of apostolic missions.

Simpson's lessons from Acts for the church of his day are a challenge to The Christian and Missionary Alliance a century later. Although Acts is descriptive, not prescriptive, it illustrates in history God's divine intention for the church. History is real. It is the three-dimensional activity of our Spirit God, and we must pursue our quest for identity and integrity with His working.

The lessons Simpson drew from the book of Acts raise an important issue. If world evangelization is the supreme business of the church, and if a solid home base is the essential foundation for effective missionary work, then, as Simpson observes, the preparation of a missionary church is most relevant. It was Jesus' primary concern in His high-priestly prayer in John 17. In fact, that prayer provides us profound insight into the ministry role of the ascended and enthroned Christ as Mediator and Head of the church.

Jesus Prayed for the Church

Jesus was facing a transition from His earthly work to His heavenly, and He appears to move into an inner sanctum of holy ground as though the temple veil was already rent. The solemn recognition of what immediately lay before Him makes His prayer almost too sacred for human analysis, yet it reveals for us the primary essence of His heavenly role.

In the shadow of the cross and in completion of His earthly ministry (17:4), Jesus prays for the protection of His embryonic church in a world dominated by the evil one (17:11–16). He prays for a special unity among His disciples in prescience of the mission He has given them.

This unity and the mission that is to flow from it have a direct relation to the mediatorial ministry He now occupies at the Father' right hand (17:17–19).

Jesus repeats two entreaties. The first is for sanctification. "Sanctify them by the truth; your word is truth" (17:17). Again, "For them I sanctify myself, that they too may be truly sanctified" (17:19). Jesus sanctified His union with the Father that His disciples might be sanctified in union with Him: "I in them and you in me. May they be brought to complete unity to let the world know that you sent me and have loved them even as you have loved me" (17:23). Jesus' full identification with the Father directly parallels the disciples' intended identification with Christ. It is a sanctified relationship.

The second entreaty Jesus repeats is directly associated with His first. He asks that this sanctified relationship might penetrate the world. "As you sent me into the world, I have sent them into the world" (17:18). Again, "My prayer is not for them alone.l pray also for those who will believe in me through their message, that all of them may be one, Father, just as you are in me and I am in you. May they also be in us so that the world may believe that you have sent me" (17:20–21).

The celestial purpose of this sanctifying union that Christ anticipates between Himself in His heavenly position and His church in its earthly position is world evangelization: "I in them and you in me. May they be brought to complete unity to let the world know that you sent me and have loved them even as you have loved me" (17:23). Inward sanctification was to result in outward ministry to the world.

The Church: A Global Expression of Christ

This global intent in the core relationship Jesus sees between His church and Himself epitomizes His intercession. Coming soon after He instituted the communion table, Jesus' prayer anticipates the new organic union His death and resurrection will make possible. The transition from His present position on earth to the right hand of the Father in the heavenlies had implications so significant that he prayed: "For them I sanctify myself, that they too may be truly sanctified" (17:19). Jesus' obedience in suffering was facing its most critical hour.

In God's mind, union between Jesus, in His glorified position, and His disciples on earth was pivotal to everything creation and redemption were about. Jesus' fulfilled obedience would make this union possible in order that the whole world might receive the Good News. He was to be "lifted up" on the cross "so that everyone who believes in him may have eternal life" (John 3:14–15).

The cross has a cosmic position. Its grandeur and scope for redemption transcends Israel as a nation. It comprehends the whole earth. This fact the soon-to-be-born church is to realize. The church's faith for ministry is to be sized and formulated by the dimensions of the cross.

At Jesus' ascension 500 followers heard Him declare, "All authority in heaven and on earth has been given to me. Therefore go and make disciples of all nations. . . . And surely I will be with you always, to the very end of the age" (Matthew 28:18–20). But these followers, conditioned as they were by their cultural background, could not readily absorb the full meaning of Jesus' words. Only as they received and obeyed the Holy Spirit, only as God's providence led them would their spiritual and physical horizons expand to assimilate the scope and reality of Christ's kingdom work. For this the disciples needed to be sanctified, even as Jesus sanctified Himself.

During the 40 days between His resurrection and ascension, Jesus on one occasion commanded His apostles not to leave Jerusalem until they had received the gift of the Holy Spirit. The gift of the Spirit would empower them to be His "witnesses in Jerusalem, and in all Judea and Samaria, and to the ends of the earth" (Acts 1:8). To us in our shrunken world of jet aircraft and communication satellites, the challenge may seem plausible. In that first century, Jesus' words must have been mind-blowing, unreal.

The slowness with which Jesus' followers grasped His global intent is documented by the book of Acts. It took the intense persecution following Stephen's martyrdom (Acts 7) to dislodge the church from Jerusalem into "Judea and Samaria" (8:1). Eventually some of them reached "Phoenicia, Cyprus and Antioch," but even then their witness was "only to Jews" (11:19).

Peter's problem with the vision God gave him in Joppa (10:9–17) and the debate in Jerusalem after Cornelius, a Gentile, and his household embraced the Christian faith (11:1–18) further exemplifies the church's slowness to grasp its worldwide responsibility. Only after the largely Gentile congregation in Antioch, prompted by the Holy Spirit, sends forth its senior pastors, Barnabas and Paul, as missionaries does the church begin to understand its global nature and function (13:1–3).

Authority and Union

Jesus Christ's global agenda demands not only that the church accept His authoritative position but perceive its corporate and organic union with Him in His mediatory role. These two concepts should and must totally condition the church's ministry. With the descent of the Holy Spirit at Pentecost, Jews from almost every Roman ethnic province miraculously heard the gospel in their own tongue— some 14 languages, at least.

Assuredly this demonstrated not only God's global intention for the gospel but a fellowship potential that bridges wide cultural differences. Jesus' high-priestly prayer was in anticipation of this. Jesus' same mediatory ministry has continued for nearly 2,000 years: "[Jesus] is able to save completely those who come to God through him, because he always lives to intercede for them" (Hebrews 7:25).

Christ's continuing ministry of intercession for His church is the intensive purpose of God the Father to bring salvation to the whole world. The Spirit who proceeds from the Father and is a part of the Son's intercessory ministry (Romans 8:27) is also at work in the hearts of believers, urging them to respond to God's purpose and to enter into the fellowship of Christ's suffering. He assures us that "in all things God works for the good of those who love him, who have been called according to his purpose" (8:28). The primary focus of this promise is the corporate church (not isolated individuals, as we so often apply it) and encompasses "all things" the church does.

The highest good of those who love God is to fulfill His purpose in Christ through the church (8:29). Only in the process of obedience and faith can the church learn the authority and sufficiency of Christ. Mankind, by his own ability and wisdom never is prepared to fulfill God's plan. The church, regrettably, has been slow to size its faith and function in divine terms. The mediating ministry of Christ and the Spirit's empowering ministry within the church are intended to make the church a colaborer with Christ in global redemption. Only thus will the church be coheir with Christ. Only as it suffers with Christ will the church reign with Christ.

The Church: A Strategic Expression of Christ

Only God could have pictured the New Testament church as an agency for world redemption. He began the church in Jerusalem, a specific—and very significant—locality. The church had to prove the effectiveness of the gospel in Jerusalem if it was to exercise faith to take it forth universally. There in Jerusalem the composite body, not isolated individuals, began to sense the *pleroma*—the plenitude, the fullness— of the glorified Christ who was "appointed . . . to be head over everything for the church, which is his body" (Ephesians 1:22–23).

God acted upon a particular praying body of believers at Jerusalem when he filled them with His Holy Spirit and enabled them to declare "the wonders of God" (Acts 2:11) in at least 14 non-Aramaic languages. He acted again

51

upon a particular praying body of believers at Antioch when He directed the leaders, "Set apart for me Barnabas and Saul for the work to which I have called them" (13:2).

Peter, singly, could not fully grasp the mighty vision, either at Pentecost or at Joppa. Paul, singly, could not totally grasp it in his encounter with the risen Jesus on the road to Damascus, not even when Ananias prophesied that he would be God's "chosen instrument to carry my name before the Gentiles and their kings and before the people of Israel" (9:15). Only through the corporate church and the fullness of Christ in the church could the commanding vision be understood.

Syrian Antioch was where it began. Antioch, as it relates to the Christian church, has several distinctions. It was the first city where Gentiles purposely were evangelized (Acts 11:20). At Antioch the believers were first called Christians (11:26). Antioch was where Paul first gained prominence as a church leader (13:1). Antioch was also the first New Testament church to send forth church planting, career missionaries (13:2–3). But all of this developed gradually.

When the church in Jerusalem heard that Gentiles had turned to Christ Jesus in Antioch, it sent Barnabas to investigate (11:20–22). He in turn was led to seek out Paul. But not at once. First he had to see "the evidence of the grace of God" (11:23) in the racially mixed fellowship. He also waited until "a great number of people were brought to the Lord" (11:24).

And before the Holy Spirit prompted the church leaders in Antioch to send forth the first missionaries, the church had at the very least a full year of concentrated teaching by Barnabas and Paul. During that year, the church developed prophets and teachers of its own. So it was to an established, mature church that the Holy Spirit gave directions, "Set apart . . . Barnabas and Saul for the work to which I have called them" (13:2). Missions was the result of obeying Christ's Great Commission: making disciples by baptizing them and teaching them to fully obey all that Jesus had commanded.

Where Did the Apostles Go?

The inspired New Testament record makes no effort after Pentecost to follow the ministry of all of Jesus' apostles. (Peter, John and Paul are the exceptions.) Rather, it describes the church developing in ministry. The church recognized Peter as appointed particularly to the Jews and Paul to the Gentiles (Galatians 2:7). Peter worked from Jerusalem, Paul from Antioch. Tradition puts John as bishop over the seven churches of Asia Minor addressed in Revelation 2 and 3, the longest surviving of Christ's immediate apostles.

The writings of Hegesippus and Eusebius inform us that Thomas labored in India, Philip in Phrygia, Simon Zelotes in Egypt, Andrew in Greece, Matthias in Ethiopia, Judas Thaddeus in Persia, Bartholomew in Armenia. Had God's intent been missions per se, the exploits of these other apostles might well have occupied divine revelation. But God's design was evangelization through the *church*, the body of Christ, gifted and called.

Thus Acts, written by Luke, Paul's faithful associate, and the Letters written by Paul, Peter and John—describing and guiding the church's development and ministry— comprise the "God-breathed" New Testament Scriptures that He has given us "for teaching, rebuking, correcting and training in righteousness" (2 Timothy 3:16) that the church of Jesus Christ may be thoroughly equipped for every good work. The church—Christ's "body, the fullness of him who fills everything in every way" (Ephesians 1:22)—is God's primary agency for the global advancement of the gospel. Although leaders and missionaries are very necessary, missions must have a home base: disciples who are united to Christ and to each other. The church, and nothing less, is the strategic global expression of Christ and His gospel.

In her failure to fulfill God's calling, Israel had degraded her view of the transcendent God to that of a tribal deity such as the surrounding nations worshiped. The church, in its local expression, is not to be a mere ethnic enclave; it represents Christ as Lord and Sovereign in a universe of people. Though ethnic homogeneity may be helpful to local church growth and may serve to solidify its unity, the church in its maturation is destined to rise to a unity in Christ that transcends ethnicity. "God does not show favoritism," Jewish Peter said to Gentile Cornelius and his gathered household. The church is to reach out to the whole world without bias or prejudice.

The book of Revelation depicts Christ in the midst of the seven golden lampstands, representing the seven churches (2:1). Every church has a strategic identity and corporate responsibility, as indicated by specific commendations and judgments. But the scenes of visions move from the individual church to its final gathering to Christ. Revelation projects Jesus Christ Himself as approaching His final coronation. In that dramatic event, He alone is found worthy to receive the sealed book from God Almighty seated on the throne. The scroll seems to be a final revelation for judgment. The whole weight of the Scriptures is to be disclosed to the world.

In celestial preparation, the four "living creatures" and the 24 elders sing:

> *"You are worthy to take the scroll*
> *and to open its seals,*
> *because you were slain,*
> *and with your blood you purchased men*
> *for God*
> *from every tribe and language and people*
> *and nation."*
> (Revelation 5:9)

"Every tribe and language and people and nation." God's purview is worldwide. God's purpose for the church is worldwide evangelization. When the book of Revelation comes to its final close, as we noted earlier, its call is to "whoever"—"whoever is thirsty," "whoever wishes" (22:17). Jesus is the Living Water that the "whoevers" of our earth thirst for (see John 4:10). God has made His saved people—the church—the reservoir of that Living Water (4:14). Woe to the church if it fails to make Jesus available to those who need Him.

The Church: A Sanctified Expression of Christ

As we earlier observed, Jesus' high priestly prayer that the disciples might be truly sanctified (John 17) was a prescience of Christ's present mediatorial intercession. Although sin was the important factor in the reconciliation Jesus purchased on Calvary, the sanctification Jesus prayed for was not of necessity a problem of sin. Jesus had no sin when He sanctified Himself (17:19). Neither was He necessarily dealing with a sin problem when He prayed that His disciples might be "truly sanctified" (17:19).

In salvation Jesus provides not merely a righteous standing, or relationship. He provides also an intimacy often illustrated in Scripture by marriage. There is an intimacy of relationship that determines the family as God has ordained it. Similarly, there is a spiritual intimacy of sanctification ordained by God for His "household" (Ephesians 2:19), the church. This powerful bond transcends racial, social, linguistic and cultural barriers. Jesus implied as much when He said, "My prayer is not for [my disciples] alone. I pray also for those who will believe in me through their message, that all of them may be one, Father, just as you are in me and I am in you. May they also be in us so that the world may believe that you have sent me" (17:20–21).

The "Just-as-you-are-in-me-and-I-am-in-you" relationship between Jesus and the Father is also projected between Jesus and His church. This is not to be occasional. Rather, it is a lifestyle that Jesus experienced with the

Father, through the Spirit, during His whole ministry on earth.

Simpson was convinced that without an intelligent faith in Christ as Sanctifier, neither the church's local ministry nor its missionary efforts would be effective. The contrast Jesus drew between a house built on sand and one built on rock (Matthew 7:24–27) was predicated on the assumption that winds and floods were sure to come. But, He promised, "the gates of Hades will not overcome [my church]" (Matthew 16:18).

Unless the power of God is providentially and continuously at work in His sanctified church, missionary work is an impossible task. Missions is dependent on an essential core of Spirit-filled people who find in their union with Christ the authority and dynamic for expansion. Paul cautioned those who succeeded him in missionary ministry to build on the foundation of Christ Himself, the Foundation he already had laid as a wise masterbuilder. He knew that whatever was built ultimately would be tested by fire (1 Corinthians 3:12–15).

How Firm the Foundation?

Missionaries represent the home church in its responsibility to Jesus' Great Commission. They are reproducing a foundation already laid. And unless that home foundation is firm, their efforts to plant churches in "the regions beyond" will fail. The longer the tent cords (to accommodate more canvas), the stronger must be the stakes (Isaiah 54:2).

Referring to the church at Antioch (Acts 13), Simpson urges: "Let us, therefore, not forget that it is God's plan to send missionaries from a home center. The idea of independent missions apart from that supporting center is not scriptural. There must be two ends to the work, the home and the foreign, both equally responsive and helping."[2] In the mind of Simpson, this supporting center was not essentially financial or organizational but spiritual. He considered a center of deeper life commitment strategically necessary.

When God calls His church to dedicated service with a global vision, it is not to the neglect or the weakening of its local ministry. If this were so, God would not in all things be working "for the good of those who love him, who have been called according to his purpose" (Romans 8:28). Indeed, the missionary mandate begins at home—at "Jerusalem" (Luke 24:47; Acts 1:8). But the power and working of God involve its total ministry—in Jerusalem and to the ends of the earth. Consequently, the home church firmly convinced of Christ's authority and full sufficiency becomes the beneficiary of the larger blessing. It cannot suffer loss. This truth is basic to the kind of faith that will accomplish the Great Commission.

Repeat: The Scriptures portray the local church as representing the Lord in His enthroned glory, whose redemptive fullness has cosmic dimensions (Colossians 1:19–20). The church, structured and motivated by this conviction, will envision Christ as Head over all things to the church, both to fill its members with His Spirit and "to fill the whole universe" (Ephesians 1:22–23; 4:10). When this truth is demonstrated in body-life, the church will be spiritually dynamic in its total working. Such maturity of mind and motivation is only attained through the Sanctifier. Sanctification produces union with Christ and with fellow believers.

The Strategic Church at Rome

Paul seems to have regarded the church in Rome as a world missionary center. Although it was a church he had not planted and had not seen, he carried a deep desire to minister to its members (Romans 1:15). His goal was to reach Spain with the gospel, and he wanted the church to be involved with him in the task (Romans 15:24).

Paul ends his letter to the Romans with this benediction:

Now to him who is able to establish you by my gospel and the proclamation of Jesus Christ, according to the revelation of the mystery hidden for long ages past, but now revealed and made known through the prophetic writings by the command of the eternal God, so that all nations might believe and obey him—to the only wise God be glory forever through Jesus Christ! Amen. (16:25–27)

It is strange to hear Paul writing about "my gospel" when he has warned the Galatians against "turning to a different gospel" (Galatians 1:6) other than the one God has revealed. But Paul's benedictory thought in relation to what he previously has covered in his letter clarifies his meaning. Members of the church at Rome needed to be established more securely in their gospel proclamation. The "mystery hidden for long ages past" had at last been exposed by fuller revelation. The command of the eternal God, when observed in the full light of the entire prophetic writings, is that "all nations might believe and obey him."

Paul's ministry "in these regions" from which he wrote was complete (15:23). For many years he had longed to visit the believers in Rome. What better time than on his planned trip to Spain? Evidently Paul felt the church in Rome needed further training as a missionary church. He sensed, too, their need for grounding in foundational doctrine: sin as a universal and fatal malady (Romans 1–3); a settled salvation through justification (4–5), sanctification through identification with Christ's death and resurrection (6–8). Importantly, the church needed to recognize Israel's failure in its calling and mission to the world—a failure the church should not repeat (9-11). It needed to know the importance of the spiritual gifts to its calling and mission (12:1–15:6). Then it should boldly proclaim the universality of redemption that so gloriously included them and him (15:7–22). Finally, he would show them how they might practically share in his calling and ministry (15:23–33).

The church entrusted with a gospel of global dimension proclaims the Lord and His sovereign fullness. This greatly diminishes all the nitty-gritty concerns of the local church because Christ, the Head of the body, the church, demands in everything to have the supremacy (Colossians 1:18).

The Church: A Commissioned Expression of Christ

Just as worship, fellowship, nurture, training and evangelism are to involve the whole church, so is its missionary mandate. This was exemplified at Antioch. Paul and Barnabas first related to the Antioch church as pastors and teachers (Acts 11:26; 13:1). Later, they became the church's missionaries (13:2–3; 14:26–27). The Antioch church's worldwide mission was an extension of the church. When Gentile converts (won by their missionaries) were discriminated against by Judaizers, leaders from Antioch met in Jerusalem with church leaders there. The need was to establish union between Gentile and Jewish believers so as to give universal free course to the gospel (Acts 15:1–35). Missions is a corporately based, commissioned ministry.

Local churches tend always to reproduce their own counterparts in missionary church-planting. In promising His disciples His presence and assuring them of His full and complete authority in heaven and on earth, our Lord intended a reproductive process: in going to make disciples of nations by baptizing and by teaching, the apostles would establish churches capable in turn of establishing more reproducing churches.

Meanwhile, as the book of Acts indicates, the planting of churches in new frontiers went on simultaneously. The task of evangelism and disciple-making overlaps with the task of missions, but the two are not synonymous. Church planting and church growth, qualitatively and quantitatively, should be the outcome of both.

As with Israel of the Old Testament, so with the church in the New: God has covenanted with a peoplehood to carry out His universal plan and purpose of redemption. The church's task is not finished until witnesses in the form of churches are reproduced among all nations. This seems clear when Jesus' statement in Matthew 24:14 about the gospel being preached in all nations as a witness is joined with His parable of the traveling householder in Mark 13:34.

The potential fulfillment of Jesus' high-priestly prayer is seen in the apostolic methods of ministry in Acts. Church planting around the world among all nations is God's plan and the effectiveness of this is anticipated through the church's vital union with Christ and its members with each other.

The church growth movement, founded by the late Donald A. McGavran, has had a strong and generally fortuitous influence on The Christian and Missionary Alliance. McGavran expressed its principal theorem in these words:

> Faithfulness in multiplying churches nourished on the Bible and full of the Holy Spirit is a sine qua non to carrying out the purposes of God. . . . Churches multiplying across the world in every nation demonstrate that a new era has begun. Like the Holy Spirit, they are an earnest of the triumphant reign of God which, in His good time, will be brought in by Him.[3]

Wanted: Churches Motivated for Missions

The church's true nature emerges in her engagement with the world locally and universally. Its faith and style of body-life are shaped by its obedience to the Head of the church and through its relationship with His plan and supernatural working. The church does not operate as a storage battery, soaking up power against future demand. The church becomes God's instrument by relational function. It is sustained moment by moment by the resurrection life of the enthroned Christ, who holds the church in solemn allegiance. Christ Himself unites its powers in a pattern of self-giving that demonstrates the church's union with Him who has universal power and authority.

The Alliance Constitution, Article II regarding objectives, states that the Alliance "is committed to world missions, stressing the fullness of Christ in personal experience, building the church and preaching the gospel to the ends of the earth."[4] The early church's missionary method was to plant churches and to motivate them to missions. Churches established by missionary effort became self-supporting, self-propagating and self-governing. Missionary teams were "foundation lay-ers" of indigenous churches.

Paul described his modus operandi explicitly: "To be a minister of Christ Jesus to the Gentiles with the priestly duty of proclaiming the gospel of God, so that the Gentiles might become an offering acceptable to God, sanctified by the Holy Spirit. Therefore I glory in Christ Jesus in my service to God. . . . It has always been my ambition to preach the gospel where Christ was not known, so that I would not be building on someone else's foundation" (Romans 15:16–17, 20). For Paul to identify himself as a foundation-lay-er on new ground clearly implies an evangelism that results in the building of churches.

Furthermore, Paul expected his apostolic ministry to increase as the churches he planted were built up and became motivated for missions. To the Corinthian church he wrote: "Our hope is that, as your faith continues to grow, our area of activity among you will greatly expand, so that we can preach the gospel in the regions beyond you. For we do not want to boast about work already done in another man's territory" (2 Corinthians 10:15–16). Paul anticipated his apostolic motivation would so prepare the Corinthian church that the gospel could be preached to more distant regions. Thus both his own activity and that of the Corinthian congregation would greatly expand.

The Scriptures reflect a strong contingency between the church as a strategic base and the missionary expansion of the gospel. Missions is a mutual task. The local church must be as committed to missions as the missionary must be committed to his home church. Apostolic or missionary motivation is not confined to missionaries. The stronger the motivation in the home church, the more power and authority will be manifested both in the church and in the task of missions.

The Lord Himself is Head of the church wherever true believers come together for mutual edification and to serve the Triune God. Indigenous responsibility is the same at home or abroad, in "Jerusalem" or in the "uttermost parts."

Essentially, missions is an identification of need and a divine strategy. It is to hear the voice of God concerning those bereft of the gospel and among whom no national or "people-group" witness has been established. Some of these people-groups are in North America among the tens of thousands of recent immigrants.

That people are lost except through the salvation Christ offers is the key to both evangelism and missions. But that there are those who have not heard the gospel in their "heart language" and do not have access to a viable church or possibly even the Scriptures, is a condition for which existing churches have a primary responsibility. Jesus' commission to disciple all nations requires a strategy to penetrate nations by planting churches in the manner of John, Peter and Paul.

The primary responsibility of believers is always in relation to their home church. The Lordship of Christ in their lives and in the life of the churches to which they belong cannot be separated. This is as true for missionaries as for local church members. Missions must have a home base. Missions is an extension of what the home church is in vision, faith and obedience. As a priority within the church it reflects most directly the Lord in His sovereign fullness and His own self-giving for world redemption.

Missions is also the daystar of Christ's return. The discipleship process of a missionary church thus will reflect a willingness to depend on Christ to fulfill His universal plan and purpose through His people in anticipation of His coming. Missions is more than a mere expediency or an added responsibility. Rather, it fits a comprehensive plan and purpose for which total preparedness becomes the highest challenge.

Endnotes

[1] A.B. Simpson, "Back to Antioch," *The Alliance Weekly* (March 13, 1913), pp. 371ff. The seven lessons, abbreviated from Simpson's article, form an instructive insight into his ecclesiology.

[2] A.B. Simpson, *Christ in the Bible*, Vol. XVI (Harrisburg, PA: Christian Publications, Inc., n.d.), p. 37.

[3] Quoted by Malcolm K. Bradshaw in *Church Growth through Evangelism in Depth* (Pasadena, CA: William Carey Library, 1969), p. 14.

[4] *Manual of The Christian and Missionary Alliance*, 1989 edition, p. 3. Available through the National Office, P.O. Box 35000, Colorado Springs, CO 80935-3500.

4

The Structure of a Missionary Church

*T*he organization of a missionary church necessarily follows spiritual preparation. To be fully relevant to our generation, the structure of the church must serve its spiritual mandate. Unless the church is practical to our task-oriented age of technology and makes provision for the priesthood ministry of every member, it is not ready to obey fully Christ's Great Commission. Structure must serve the gospel and meet the challenge of the age we live in.

"The age we live in," wrote Simpson almost 80 years ago, "is one of deep solemnity and crisis." He continues:

Everything in it points to a speedy and transcendently important consummation, and the Holy Scriptures meet this expectation with the clearest intimations of the personal and premillennial coming of the Lord Jesus Christ to set up His kingdom on the earth and bring in 'the restitution of all things.' . . .

God is calling us as never before to look on the fields, for they are white to the harvest, and go into all the world in this present generation and preach the gospel to every creature. Are not these distinctive truths in which we can all unite without fanaticism and, in the joy and power of a full salvation, go forth to save a dying generation of one thousand millions and prepare for the close of the world's most marvelous century and the coming of the Lord Himself in His kingdom and glory?[1]

Such words from another generation have a peculiar ring of relevance as we close the century that Simpson spoke of. They bring to mind the words of Paul: "The hour has come for you to wake up from your slumber, because our salvation is nearer now than when we first believed" (Romans 13:11).

Spiritual Nature Determines Structure

As we have noted, the theology of the church historically has focused more on structure to meet local or immediate needs than on the church's scriptural nature. The Protestant Reformation was a reaction to the papal and hierarchical structure of the Roman Catholic Church. The primary issues of doctrine thus centered on salvation by grace through faith, the authority of the Word and the priesthood of the believer. Teaching concerning the church itself focused mostly on functional survival and religious establishment rather than on the Lord's Great Commission for the church. The *ecclesia*—the "gathering"—was structured to strengthen the Protestant cause against overwhelming odds.

The church constantly is called upon to rethink its faith under changing circumstances and needs. But in the aftermath of the Reformation, ecclesiology became formalized in terms of church/state relations and how leadership authority might be expressed over a territory or between churches. Since then, Protestant churches have traditionally been categorized structurally as episcopal, presbyterian or congregational.

While structure has important implications, Scripture gives little reference to it. The church exists to proclaim and represent the gospel. "The New Testament is concerned wholly with the church—" argued Louis L. King, past president of The Christian and Missionary Alliance at a conference of evangelical missions leaders, "not with the organizational structure of the church but with its nature and function." King saw the church as a living organism infused with life from its Head (Ephesians 1:22–23) and destined to be God's agency to carry the gospel to the ends of the earth (Acts 1:8).[2]

In Alliance thought, organization has been guided by a pragmatic principle: obedience to the Great Commission. Churches are organisms—people organized to represent "the body of Christ" in local communities around the world. Theoretically, such thinking regarding the local church demands an understanding of the church as a peoplehood having particular gifts for service with a divine purpose and objective. In other words, nature and function should determine organization, not the other way around. As a people with relational gifts, the early church was courageous and vigorous. Its leaders were flexible, its style was simple and practical. The early church was not muscle-bound by over-organization. But neither was it impotent for lack of order and structure.

The Local Church's Need for Structure

Although the church is primarily an organism—the body of Christ—it is also an organization. As the human body is not only flesh and blood but a skeletal structure as well, so the church. All believers are called to be members of a local church and commissioned to participate actively in carrying the gospel into all the world. This is a founding conviction of the Alliance and represents its basic operational philosophy.

According to Ephesians 4:11, the Lord has appointed special leadership gifts: apostles, prophets, evangelists and pastor-teachers. In the Scriptures the church is also described as having elders (Acts 11:30; 20:17), deacons and deaconesses (Philippians 1:1; Romans 16:1–2) and women in ministry (Romans 16:3, 6, 12; Philippians 4:2–3).

The church had stated meetings (1 Corinthians 16:2). To consider special issues it held councils to which churches sent representatives (Acts 15:2). The decisions of the council in turn were communicated with constituted authority to regional local churches (Acts 15:22–23). Converts to the Christian faith were baptized (Acts 2:41; 8:12). The Lord's Supper was observed in ceremonial order (1 Corinthians 11:33–34). There is instruction concerning spiritual gifts, which must be corporately recognized and treated with discretion and orderliness (1 Corinthians 12, 14). All these offices, appointments and observances imply organization.

Organization, however, tends to functionalize an organism. Any liberty carried to license evokes disgust and even pain. Liberty is only possible in the shadow of authority, which in turn necessitates some form of organization so that the purposes and objectives of the body may be fulfilled. Principles of purpose determine principles of organization. Spiritual maturity demands maturity in government, finances, programming, propagation, nurture and training. It is reflected in the church's relations to missions, to other churches and to the community at large. All of this is inherent in the spiritual nature and function of the church.

Making disciples by developing maturity in worshipful service and efficient relationships is basic to missionary effectiveness. Only what the church grows locally can it hope to transplant abroad. As the local church focuses on disciple-making, Christ promises it His presence and authority in taking the gospel to all the world.

Structuring for Missionary Involvement

All believers within a local church are commissioned to participate actively in carrying the gospel into all the world. This is a founding conviction of The Christian and Missionary Alliance. Making disciples by developing maturity in worshipful service is basic to missionary effectiveness.

Missiologist James Scherer has observed that since the fourth century, missions has been considered something quite distinct from the mainstream of church life.[3] As a consequence of this segregation, some argue that independent missionary agencies are the best hope for facilitating missions on behalf of the church.

The Alliance, however, since its founding and despite its beginnings as an interdenominational missionary society, has taken issue with such a philosophy. It has contended without apology that missions is the heart and soul of the church of Jesus Christ. The church is God's cosmic agency for proclaiming the gospel. The church's scope must be as great as the all-sufficient Christ who is the church's Head. Alliance structure, therefore, has developed in the belief that missions is an essential function of the church.

When a church believes that all its members are God's agents for world evangelization, that church is placed in a unique position. Local churches nurtured by the Word and full of the Holy Spirit are God's ordained means for world evangelization. The Scriptures describe the church as "the pillar and foundation of the truth" (1 Timothy 3:15), a body of spiritual members over whom Christ, as sovereign Savior and Sanctifier, is the Head (Colossians 1:18).

While churches function at different levels of maturity and are conditioned by the culture and circumstances in which they minister, each represents Christ's body in a particular place, and each is positioned with a whole-world outlook. Thus the church, convinced of its place in God's program and united in faith through the discipline of God's Word, will not fall prey to satanic attack or become ineffective in its ministry.

For the Local Church, for the Denomination

Christ's authority and presence inherent in His Commission to the church (Matthew 28:18–20) applies both to the local church and to the fellowship of churches. In 1978, when the General Council of The Christian and Missionary Alliance set centennial goals for 1987, the Board of Managers was commissioned to determine the principles by which the goals were to be achieved. The first principle adopted reads this way:

> We believe that the glory of God and the highest good of Alliance churches are best served by a structure in which there is a place for local churches, districts and headquarters to cooperate at every stage. We believe that a cooperative effort at all levels provides the greatest assurance of spiritual freedom and success.[4]

By this principle the Board was saying that the districts and headquarters exist for the service of Alliance churches. The churches, in turn, exist for the service of the denomination and for the evangelical church at large. Local churches, however, are the primary agents for the furtherance of the gospel. Mainly it is through the church that converts are made, discipled and brought to maturity.

It is also through the local church that prayer and money are generated and recruits enlisted for Christian service. The local church is not a pawn moved by outside players, but neither should it be a law unto itself. The local church commissions, the local church legislates constituted authority, and the local church submits to that authority. This organized authority, in turn, is accountable to implement effective extension of the gospel at home and worldwide.

Church authority is always derived first from the Lord through the apostolic Word, then from its commissioned leaders who administrate the united efforts of the churches. Simpson advocated great strength at the center of the organization and great freedom in local church function. He likened this to the federal system of the United States Government.[5]

The principle was expressed this way in 1978:

> We believe there is true ingenuity in each church and district to devise the best, the most economical, the most efficient way to achieve the goals. We believe that the headquarters' responsibility is to make sure that the people's desire as expressed in Council action is properly understood—that the necessary options are thoroughly evaluated before a plan is promulgated. We believe that headquarters' role is to set the criteria, give suggestions and help provide resources in personnel and finances to assist churches and districts to achieve their goals.[6]

These considerations regarding the function of the church reflect Alliance structure. Because Christ is represented within the local church, representative leaders of those churches, convening at the Annual Council, give input to denominational leaders. Responsible participation by churches is therefore important. Denomination and district leaders develop principles from the input of local churches, thus assuring total participation. Organizational dynamics, when fully grasped, avoids much misunderstanding and fosters mutual confidence and encouragement.

If any Alliance church supposes it exists to blindly serve the district or the denomination, the comprehensive modus operandi of the Alliance has not been properly communicated to that church. In fact, the exact reverse is true. The district and the national office exist specifically to serve the local churches as they fulfill their evangelistic mandate locally and worldwide.

The Local Church in the Denominational Structure

The denomination exists for the local church's benefit and larger ministry. Many endeavors cannot be carried out by the local church acting alone. For example, the education and training of missionaries and pastors can seldom be done efficiently by the local church. So also the overseeing of their ordination, their placement, their discipline of service. In missionary work, few local churches are in a position to develop strategy, administer communications and promotion, encourage overseas church leaders in church propagation. These and numerous other functions are best rendered by leadership at the district and denominational levels.

Whatever the level of leadership, a servant attitude is requisite. All service is best accomplished as we submit to one another "out of reverence for Christ" (Ephesians 5:21).

In keeping with the "Jerusalem-Judea-Samaria-ends-of-the-earth" pattern described by Jesus (Acts 1:8), the Alliance has developed creative principles of structure for church growth. Churches plant churches in their regions, missionaries delegated and commissioned by home churches plant churches in other nations. Autonomous national churches in turn become missionary. A non-legislative alliance of these autonomous national churches meets quadrennially to learn from one another and to inspire each other.

Creative methods like this are best accomplished within a structure of harmony and under capable leaders. At the same time, none of it can happen unless local churches—at home and abroad—are becoming pillars and foundations of truth (1 Timothy 3:15) and the process of discipling is carried out by those local churches in consecrated service. Strong mutual trust at all levels strengthens the total ministry. Nothing undermines the Lord's work more quickly than mutual distrust. It is the sign of a weak union in Christ Jesus.

Fellowship in the gospel and a deepening discipleship come as faith matures. Faith in Christ and full dedication to His service always result in wholesome ways by which God's people relate to each other. God's Word exhorts us to "leave the elementary teachings about Christ and go on to maturity" (Hebrews 6:1). Jesus' command to disciple-making is through a twofold process: by baptizing and by teaching the convert "to observe everything I have commanded you" (Matthew 28:19–20). In the Alliance, emphasis on the deeper life and missions historically has characterized its discipling process. These distinctives shape not only the function of the local church but the local church's relationship to its district, to the denomination and to the evangelical church at large.

The Local Church and the Missionary Mandate

The big picture dictates the detail and proportion an artist brings to the canvas. In the church, God's ultimate purpose determines the church's methods. Jesus alluded to this principle when He commented on the "pagans'" preoccupation with life's material essentials such as food and clothing. He said to His followers, "Seek first [God's] kingdom and his righteousness, and all these things will be given to you as well" (Matthew 6:33). Putting the priority on God's ultimate purpose is something like preventive medicine. It helps us keep the structure healthy and on target. Understanding God's ultimate purpose, therefore, is essential for determining church-mission methodology.

The most complete letter on the doctrine of the church is Ephesians. Believed to have been an encyclical to a number of churches, the letter is replete with expressions about God's ultimate purpose.

In chapter one Paul sets forth in explicit terms the factual content of God's purpose. Believers have been chosen "in accordance with his pleasure and will" (1:5) and "in accordance with the riches of God's grace that he lavished on us with all wisdom and understanding" (1:7–8). God has "made known to us the mystery of his will according to his good pleasure, which he purposed in Christ, to be put into effect when the times will have reached their fulfillment—to bring all things in heaven and on earth together under one head, even Christ" (1:9–10). In short, God has provided wisdom and understanding to relate all the detailed functions of the church to His one main purpose.

Against that backdrop Paul says, "I pray . . . that the eyes of your heart may be enlightened in order that you may know the hope to which [God] has called you, the riches of his glorious inheritance in the saints, and his incomparably great power for us who believe." (1:18–19). He goes on to refer to Jesus Christ: "God placed all things under his feet and appointed him to be head over everything for the church, which is his body, the fullness of him who fills everything in every way" (1:22–23).

This prayer and Paul's vision for the church are not simply ideals for planners and official church leaders. They are for every member of the church. Later Paul will say, "To each one of us grace has been given as Christ apportioned it" (4:7). In Christ's enthronement He has given the church apostles, prophets, evangelists and pastor-teachers "to prepare God's people for works of service" (4:12). In the big picture, Jesus' gifts and our service accomplish God's ultimate purpose. A time is coming when all things will be united in Christ. He is now working from the heavenlies to fulfill His kingdom purpose in and through His church.

Transforming Ideals into Reality

One purpose of structure is to move ideals and prayers toward the desired outcome. Structure shapes details and apportions resources so that God's purpose may be fulfilled. No wonder Paul prayed for enlightenment! Creative ingenuity is necessary along with faith and obedience to develop an effective structure and valid priorities.

Lack of faith and obedience result in failure to transform ideals into reality within the organized structure. This may be especially true in the church's missionary ministry. Too often the church is not organized for missions and missions is not organized for the church. Church leaders tend to gloat over generalities and spiritualities to the neglect of duty. To emphasize theory and vision without follow-through action is like faith without works. It is dead.

Denominational leaders are chosen to help organize local churches for disciple-making, for church growth and for missions. They strive to see that every believer takes the Great Commission literally. A strategy is needed if the church is to go into all the world, the world of real people. Christ has promised to return physically and personally when this gospel of the kingdom has been preached as a witness to all the world. To that end the church must be activated through structured obedience.

Although the functional significance of the local church is important to missions, the functional significance of missions for the local church is equally so. Missionary operations represent the obedience of the church to go into all the world. These missionary ministries stand accountable to the church spiritually and financially. They express the warp and woof of its very being. As missionaries are able to report their evangelistic and church-planting successes, the home constituency is encouraged to know that their cooperative service has produced a harvest and will hasten the Lord's return.

"Cast your bread upon the waters, / for after many days you will find it again" (Ecclesiastes 11:1). "Give, and it will be given to you. . . . With the measure you use, it will be measured to you" (Luke 6:38). This is a biblical principle of reciprocity that never fails. The measure given is not to be mindless casting or undisciplined giving. Rather, it is to be an obedient investment from stewards of Christ who are in turn rewarded according to their faith.

Obedience to Christ's command is the primary reason for missions. But there are others. The proper investment of our gifts to the Lord and His church is important to us. All of us one day will give an account of our stewardship. "Whoever can be trusted with very little can also be trusted with much, and whoever is dishonest with very little will also be dishonest with much. . . . If you have not been trustworthy with someone else's property, who will give you property of your own?" (Luke 16:10, 12). As believers, everything we possess is a trust from God. Our interest and responsible investing in the Lord's work determines our spiritual growth and the blessing we will bring to our church.

We would not want to be a shareholder in a company in which we had no voice and no choice of investment. But in the church, our giving too often is to random appeals over which we exercise little personal interest, prayer or intelligent participation. Our best missionary returns come as responsible church members, in a structure that serves our involvement, hear our voice of interest and welcome our participation.

The Church and Missions in Denominational Structure

Statistics seem to indicate that the church may have an erroneous impression regarding the sacrificial involvement of its members. A Gallup poll suggests that the church has fallen behind secular society in its use of volunteers. If church members are not giving three or more hours a week to the church, they are volunteering at a level below that of the general population of America.[7]

Similarly, parachurch organizations are gaining on the local church in volunteer giving and services. Unless the local church becomes more effective in recruitment and training, more convinced of its mission and more proficient in promoting and delegating ministry, increasingly it will be displaced by outside services.

Advocates of independent churches often contend that denominational structure is not biblical inasmuch as there is no precedent for it in the New Testament. Denominational organization, they insist, secularizes the church and institutionalizes it according to human ingenuity, negating the church's intended spiritual quality and freedom. But such arguments are tenuous.

The apostle Paul exercised considerable oversight of the churches he founded. He laid down rules for all the churches (1 Corinthians 7:17), and in his "concern for all the churches" (2 Corinthians 11:28) he exercised divine authority (1 Corinthians 11:16; 16:1). He left Titus in Crete so that he "might straighten out what was left unfinished and appoint elders in every town" (Titus 1:5). The church at Antioch sought the compliance of the Jerusalem church (Acts 15:1–35) inasmuch as the Jerusalem church had sent Barnabas to affirm the believers at Antioch. The council at Jerusalem appointed representatives to accompany Paul and Barnabas to Antioch to confirm the council's decisions.

Chapters 2 and 3 of Revelation seem to back the tradition that John had oversight of the seven churches of Asia Minor. We know for a fact that John rejected Diotrephes, the dictatorial usurper in one church (3 John 9). Some argue that the structured leadership evident in Acts and the Letters is descriptive, not demanded. On the other hand, it is nowhere censured. Rather, throughout the New Testament there is every evidence of a constructive, cooperative attitude toward both local and multi-church leadership. There is also evidence that the New Testament church in its numeric growth and geographic expansion transitioned from a relatively unstructured entity in Acts to a more settled one in the Letters and Revelation.

Toward an Enlarged Ministry

Structure, basically, is to allow the church an enlarged ministry. After the considerable reorganization of The Christian and Missionary Alliance in 1912, Simpson addressed the General Council with these words:

> There is one word which seems to express better than any other the peculiar processes through which the Spirit and Providence of God are leading us and teaching us at this crisis. The prayer of Epaphras in Colossians 4:12 appears to have a peculiar fitness for us at this time. Literally it may be translated, "That ye may stand perfectly adjusted in all the will of God."
>
> First, we need to be perfectly adjusted in our loyalty to Christ, and at the same time to our responsibility for the special trust which He has committed to our hands. There is a so-called loyalty to God which makes one impractical, narrow and wholly unfitted for loyal service in any human fellowship or any common cause. The apostle Paul gives us the more attractive picture of that perfect consecration of which he says, "They . . . first gave their own selves to the Lord, and unto us by the will of God." God does not want us to be afraid of losing our consecration by being true to The Christian and Missionary Alliance, by knowing how to keep rank, by marching loyally under our own standard.
>
> In the next place, we believe that our constitution and government are being adjusted to a more perfect harmony of the central authority and executive control on the one hand, and local freedom and independence in the various districts and branches on the other.[8]

If sound principles of ecclesiology are accepted, central authority and local freedom can effectively coexist. The result in Alliance ministry has been some 2,500 Alliance churches in the United States and Canada supporting world evangelization with 1,166 missionaries who serve in cooperation with 15,000 churches planted overseas. Without supporting churches, whether in North America or elsewhere, missions would not exist.

The large number of new members in Alliance churches and the still larger number of new churches over the past decade are probably two reasons for a proportional dip in Alliance giving to missions compared with overall Alliance giving. This situation calls for greater emphasis on the Alliance theology of church and mission, in the training of both our commissioned leaders and our new church members.

Simpson believed that "our foreign work is not only the fulfillment of the supreme duty of the church of Christ, but the loftiest inspiration and uplift of our whole Christian life at home."[9]

If our Alliance ecclesiology is as scripturally sound as we believe it to be, its strongest potential is yet to be discovered. Surely Christ's all-sufficiency and universal authority as Head of the church await the enlightened response of faith from Alliance churches. Paul's prayer "that the eyes of your heart may be enlightened in order that you may know the hope to which he has called you, the riches of his glorious inheritance in the saints, and his incomparably great power for us who believe" (Ephesians 1:18–19) is as appropriate today as it has ever been.

Church Structure and Missionary Dynamics

The doctrine of the church has larger implications for its structure than is generally observed. Fellowship in the gospel implies a quest in discipleship that enlarges with spiritual maturity. Disciple-making is numerically unlimited. If the process is to be continuously effective, new church members are to be taught to obey everything Jesus has commanded us (see Matthew 28:20).

The church must be structured to accommodate disciple-making as a foundational ministry. If the deeper life and missions are to be properly ingrained in our membership, the whole Bible must be taught, line upon line, precept upon precept. Strong, mature faith needs the full context of all Scripture and therefore the ministry of the Word must be well planned in both teaching and preaching.

To the immature believer missions may seem to be an extra burden meant for enthusiasts, like bird-watching or back-packing. But for mature and instructed believers, missions means serving in union with a universal Christ of history for the restitution of all things. Therefore, the mission of the local church is to bring believers into a maturity that serves Christ with a larger vision.

The apostolic mission is an integral part of Christ's church. It functions representatively in behalf of the church and is responsible to the church. As part of the church, the apostolate (meaning the missionary leaders) must identify with the church's need for faith, vision and obedience. It must understand the church's spiritual condition and, relying on the authority of the Word and the Spirit, confront the church with the opportunities before it. It must share the results of gospel proclamation and the affirmation of Christ's authority and presence as experienced by the missionary representatives. It must endeavor to increase the church's faith and confirm its obedience.

As a representative of his or her church, the missionary stands between sending and receiving churches, modeling faith and obedience. The missionary's faith in God's material supply through God's faithful people will challenge the church as a partner in service. To make this possible, the Alliance since its inception has had a furlough and tour system as a part of its missionary operation.

An annual missionary convention has become a tradition in Alliance churches, and the annual faith-promise offering (some still refer to it as the "pledge") is routine. But missionary vision and passion cannot be mere tradition. A theology of missions and a vision for missions must be renewed, strengthened and enlarged. Missions adds a climactic and finalizing dimension to everything else the church does. When the church moves with God's plan for history, missions becomes a major involvement, not a sideline.

Although missions strongly conditions Alliance structure, the importance of the local church's function is not minimized thereby, but rather enlarged. This needs to be emphasized. Local churches are not merely instrumental means for missions. They have an identity with Christ for a local ministry first—"beginning at Jerusalem." The church's mission is not simply *going;* it is *making*—making disciples. It is not simply *doing,* but *being*—it is the focus of the all-sufficient Christ in power and authority. The church's dignity and position are strengthened by faith and obedience until the more perfect image of Christ is reflected in and through its total ministry.

In His universal church God has local bodies and whole denominations quite different from The Christian and Missionary Alliance. They differ organizationally. They differ in their emphases. These differences cannot be made uniform by mere human manipulation. Christ alone builds His church. In the branch structure of the early Alliance, Simpson continually warned his constituents against the serious consequences of dividing the church and attempting to create uniformity by carnal effort. The Scriptures caution: "Make every effort to keep the unity of the Spirit through the bond of peace" (Ephesians 4:3).

When, after His resurrection, the Lord foretold that Peter would be dressed by another and made to go where by natural inclination he would not want to go, Peter asked apprehensively what would become of John. Jesus answered, "If I want him to remain alive until I return, what is that to you? You must follow me" (John 21:22). Some view differences of church orientation or denominations as a blight to the gospel, but God may view these differences as demonstrations of wideness in His mercy and kindness in His justice. We must let God be the judge.

Maybe the Lord is not particularly interested in our labels. Distinctions in church structure need not imply spiritual schism in the body of Christ. Denominations need not be likened to the "divisions" in Corinth (1 Corinthians 11:18; also 3:1–23), as one evangelical interpreter has done.[10]

Unity is not uniformity of organization. Before the Lord, each church, whether independent or denominational, must stand or fall. Some amount of structure is inevitable. It is the task of the church, in whatever form, to declare and demonstrate, pragmatically and effectively, the sovereign fullness of our Lord Jesus Christ.

Endnotes

[1] A.B. Simpson, "Distinctive Teachings," *The Alliance Weekly* (May 16, 1916), p. 326.

[2] Louis L. King, *Missions in Creative Tension*, p. 154.

[3] James Scherer, *Missionary, Go Home* (Englewood Cliffs: Prentice Hall, 1964), p. 46.

[4] Board of Managers Minutes, December 5–7, 1978, pp. 533–534.

[5] President's Report, *Annual Report to Council*, 1912.

[6] Board of Managers Minutes, op. cit.

[7] These statistics were shared at a Christian Education Leadership Conference held in Colorado Springs, Co, and reported in *The District Adult Newsletter* (C&MA), December 1991, by Daryl Dale.

[8] President's Report, op. cit.

[9]Ibid.

[10]George Eldon Ladd, *A Theology of the New Testament* (Grand Rapids: Wm. B. Eerdmans Publishing Co., 1975), p. 532.

5

Disciple-Making
in the Church

*J*esus' Great Commission (Matthew 28:18–20), spoken to a gathering of His followers after His resurrection, contains but one imperative: "Make disciples."[1] It was a charge to the church, not to individuals. Only the church is equipped to baptize converts as members of the body of Christ. Only the church is equipped to teach those baptized members all that Jesus has commanded. Only the church may claim the authority and presence of Jesus as it makes disciples in all nations.

Christ Jesus Himself laid out the course for disciple-making. The Twelve, who later became His apostles (except for Judas Iscariot), had been objects of His own discipling. Now Jesus was commissioning them and His other followers gathered on that occasion and soon to be filled with the Holy Spirit, to take up the task.

The book of Acts and the Letters are an insight as to how Jesus' first century followers carried out the commission. The early church's disciple-making was an organic continuation of the disciple-making Jesus had begun. Without that continuity, the church would not exist today.

God has appointed the church to be a continuing school of discipleship in which His divine purpose is to be fulfilled through faith, hope, love, humility and other Christ-like qualities in a peoplehood. These results come from obedience to Christ, the Master-discipler and Head of the church.

The Need for Mature Disciples

Disciple-making includes the winning of converts. But convert-making is only the beginning of what is more important: the deepening and maturing of believers to conform them to the likeness of Jesus Christ. In his book *The Body* Charles Colson expresses the church's need for what he calls a character-oriented perspective:

> This character-oriented perspective is totally foreign to our achievement-oriented society, . . . where we look at what people do rather than who they are. And it goes against everything in our consumer-oriented religious culture, where we pick and choose churches on the basis of fellowship or outreach programs or music or location or convenient parking. Rarely do we hear believers say, "I decided to join this church because of its character as a holy community." Nor do most choose a church on the basis of its capacity to disciple and equip them for ministry.
>
> Yet that should be our very first consideration. If the church is the Body, the holy presence of Christ in the

world, its most fundamental task is to build communities of holy character. And the first priority of those communities is to disciple men and women to maturity in Christ and then equip them to live their faith in every aspect of life and in every part of the world.[2]

Convert-making fails when the maturing process fails at the core of church life. "Above all else," goes one of the Proverbs, "guard your heart, / for it is the wellspring of life" (Proverbs 4:23). This is as true for the corporate church as for the individual. The first call of the church, then, is not missions or evangelism per se, but to maturity in Christ. This is what the theologians are calling discipleship formation.

The contrast between the churches in Corinth and Thessalonica illustrates the need for mature disciples in corporate church life. The church at Corinth, when Paul wrote to it, was in a stage of infancy, fragmented by immorality, divisions and uncertain leadership. The church at Thessalonica, on the other hand, while chronologically of similar age, was much farther along in spiritual maturity. The Thessalonians took discipleship seriously. "You became imitators of us and of the Lord," Paul says (1 Thessalonians 1:6).

Paul goes on to commend them for their exemplary lives: "You became a model to all the believers in Macedonia and Achaia. The Lord's message rang out from you not only in Macedonia and Achaia—your faith in God has become known everywhere" (1:7–8). Modeling maturity in body-life was basic to evangelism and missionary effectiveness. But even though the Thessalonian believers had a solid reputation, Paul exhorts them to esteem highly their leaders who worked hard at instructing and admonishing the members (5:12–13). Despite its enviable reputation, the Thessalonian church had not yet arrived. The members continued to need the anointed instruction and example of their church leaders.

Spiritual inertia and uncertain obedience were problems among the Judaic congregation addressed in the letter to the Hebrews (see Hebrews 10:32–39). Their precarious position had prompted the writer to issue a stern warning of possible impending judgment (6:4–8).

The letters to the "messengers" (pastors?) of the seven Asia Minor churches (Revelation 2, 3) warn those churches of their need for progress in maturity and discipleship.

The apostolic letters of John, Peter and Paul mainly address discipleship formation within existing churches. Although planting churches on new frontiers was Paul's first love (Romans 15:20), the main burden of his ministry was the spiritual growth of existing churches (see, for example 2 Corinthians 11:28–29; Colossians 1:9–12).

Christ and the Scriptures in Discipleship

The church's discipleship process has its center in Christ and God's Word. Not even the Holy Spirit can substitute for Christ and God's Word. Jesus Christ, revealed through the Word and by His Spirit, is the bond of union. After three years of fruitful ministry in Ephesus, Paul placed his mantle of leadership on the Ephesian elders with these words:

> You know that I have not hesitated to preach anything that would be helpful to you but have taught you publicly and from house to house. . . . I have not hesitated to proclaim to you the whole will of God. Guard yourselves and all the flock of which the Holy Spirit has made you overseers. Be shepherds of the church of God, which he bought with his own blood. . . . Now I commit you to God and to the word of his grace, which can build you up and give you an inheritance among all those who are sanctified.
>
> (Acts 20:20–32)

Paul always focuses his concern for the churches on their spiritual growth in Christ and the Word. Methods, programs or even evangelism per se are never in his purview. He sees an experiential and progressive growth of faith as the essential element in the Christian life. It is as well the essential element for the effective functioning of evangelism and missions. And what do we mean by "an experiential and progressive growth of faith"? In terms of the gospel we can call it "making disciples"—believers who follow Christ and walk with God. Because the Word of God came to the Thessalonian believers "with power, with the Holy Spirit and with deep conviction" (1 Thessalonians 1:5), the church "became a model to all the believers in Macedonia and Achaia" (1:7). From them "the Lord's message rang out" (1:8). Did not Jesus promise, "But I, when I am lifted up from the earth, will draw all men to myself" (John 12:32)?

The life, death and attested resurrection of Christ comprise a gospel with universal drawing power. The dynamics of such a gospel call for conversions. This is especially so in churches where the members are continually growing in the Lord. In such a setting new converts will not be isolated. Rather, they will be drawn into this mature nucleus from which Christ's centrality and His Word radiate to the world through preaching and personal witness. To try to substitute manipulative or entertaining programs for this is a betrayal of the gospel and its power to transform lives.

Discipleship Builds Up the Church

God's climactic purpose in giving leaders to the church is "that the body of Christ may be built up" (Ephesians 4:12). Being "built up" has a double objective: "unity in the faith and in the knowledge of the Son of God" and maturity: "attaining to the whole measure of the fullness of Christ" (4:13). Neither churches nor individual members of churches are to be "infants, . . . blown here and there by every wind of teaching" (4:14). "Instead, speaking the truth in love," they are "in all things [to] grow up into him who is the Head, that is, Christ" (4:15). Thus the entire Christian body becomes a support system that results in qualitative and quantitative growth (4:16). Disciple-making is the key to a healthy church body which, in turn, affects its community in terms of the gospel and, eventually, impacts the whole world.

It is on this premise of maturing disciples that the Scriptures anticipate world evangelization. The New Testament puts no stress on mass evangelism campaigns or programmed methods of evangelism, as helpful as they have proven to be. New Testament methodology is ultimately contingent on this one premise: a maturing discipleship within the local church. Such a body of believers is "the pillar and ground of truth" (1 Timothy 3:15).

The local church is a microcosm within the macrocosm of the universal church. It stands on its own feet, having its own identity and measure of faith. As itinerant missionaries, Paul, Silas and Timothy did not count themselves as members of any of the churches they founded. Paul wrote to the Corinthian believers:

"We are God's fellow workers; you are God's field, God's building. . . . Don't you know that you yourselves are God's temple and that God's Spirit lives in you? If anyone destroys God's temple, God will destroy him; for God's temple is sacred, and you are that temple" (1 Corinthians 3:9, 16–17). By contrasting the "we" and the "you" Paul makes it clear that he considered the Corinthian church an entity of corporate life with a resident responsibility before God.

Paul exhorts the elders at Ephesus: "Keep watch over yourselves and all the flock of which the Holy Spirit has made you overseers" (Acts 20:28). Elders and pastors need to have a deep sense of local accountability for the maturing and maturity of those within their "flock." Paul's warning against the "cunning and craftiness of men in their deceitful scheming" (Ephesians 4:14) is well taken; it continues to apply. Any threat to the fellowship is serious.

The best antidote for such infection is continued spiritual growth. Paul urges the believers to speak the truth in love and thereby "grow up into . . . Christ. From him the whole body, joined and held together by every supporting ligament, grows and builds itself up in love, as each part does its work" (4:15–16). The church has no authority but Christ. It has no source of growth, numerical or spiritual, but in Christ. From Him the whole body is to grow and responsibly build itself as a local church within the universal church of Jesus Christ.

The Role of Leaders in Discipleship

In the Lord's compassion for the multitudes, He saw people as sheep without a shepherd (Mark 6:34). Shepherdless sheep are in dire straits. So are shepherdless Christians. Indeed the Lord is our Shepherd (Psalm 23:1), but disciples within local churches also need visible leaders, people the New Testament refers to as shepherds (1 Peter 5:2; Acts 20:28). This need continues, no matter how spiritually advanced the church may be.

The church is confronted relentlessly by a hostile world and its destructive forces: humanism, secularism, atheism and other false religions. The shepherd who is going to lead, by definition must be in front of the sheep, sensing their needs, knowing the resources at their disposal. This leader, this disciple-maker, may be a pastor or a lay person. Pastors have the corporate church as their prime responsibility and should be called, trained and commissioned for their task. They must realize that all Scripture is necessary for the church's instruction. They must understand the world in which they minister, at the same time being unreservedly dependent on the Holy Spirit. Since sheep follow their leader, it is axiomatic that churches do not grow beyond the spiritual level of their pastors—a truth that pastors should regard very seriously in view of the coming day of judgment.

The most essential quality for disciple-making is faithful obedience to the Lord, whose headship over the church and whose leading by the Spirit are primary. The flow and dynamic of discipling depend heavily upon the faithfulness and vision of a church's leaders. Their obedience to the Lord and their modeling of true discipleship are essential to successful disciple-making. When discipleship breaks down at the leadership level, the whole church is affected from center to circumference.

The church serves as a school of discipleship to fulfill each member's high calling in Christ Jesus (2 Timothy 1:9; Ephesians 1:18; Philippians 3:14). Paul described a basic principle of discipleship within the church when he instructed Timothy: "The things you have heard me say in the presence of many witnesses entrust to reliable men who will also be qualified to teach others" (2 Timothy 2:2–3). The centrality of Christ and God's Word pervade the corporate image of the church, but they must be especially recognized in leadership. Merely planting churches without preparing leaders who can faithfully reproduce maturing disciples is self-defeating.

The Ingredient of Faithfulness in Discipleship

As already observed, the one most important quality for church leaders is faithfulness. Jesus asks, "Who then is the faithful and wise manager, whom the master puts in charge of his servants to give them their food allowance at the proper time? It will be good for that servant whom the master finds doing so when he returns. I tell you the truth, he will put him in charge of all his possessions" (Luke 12:42–44).

The high premium our Lord placed on faithfulness, even beyond gifts, is instructive for our day. Paul saw faithfulness as the basic strength that Christ provides: "I thank Christ Jesus our Lord, who has given me strength, that he considered me faithful, appointing me to his service" (1 Timothy 1:12). To persevere under the continuous responsibility and testings of the ministry is directly dependent upon strength that comes from the throne of divine faithfulness and grace.

Paul reminds the Corinthians: "God, who has called you into fellowship with his Son Jesus Christ our Lord, is faithful" (1 Corinthians 1:9). He addresses the Ephesian believers as "the saints in Ephesus, the faithful in Christ Jesus" (Ephesians 1:2). Likewise he calls the Colossians "the holy and faithful brothers in Christ at Colossae" (Colossians 1:2). As the marginal reading suggests, "faithful" and "believers" are the same Greek word; by definition believers are faithful.

The faithfulness that God's people have in common and God's own divine faithfulness describe true discipleship. This faithfulness is a steady walk with God, not on a treadmill but in progressive spiritual growth. Especially for those who lead, follow-through and perseverance in obedience should take precedence over the search for and exercise of spiritual gifts.

Although the New Testament puts the faithfulness of leaders and disciples above evangelism and convert-making, the church needs frequent reminders that it exists not for itself but for the needs of the world. Wise leaders must keep this perspective in mind as they teach, train and equip disciples. A preoccupation with narrow interest can blind leaders to what is ultimately significant. Such myopic vision eventuates finally in inertia and defeat. Praying for the sick, family counseling, concern for finances, program planning—these and many other ministry details have their place. But they must not cloud the leader's spiritual vision in preaching, teaching long-range direction. Faithfulness demands a consistency of vision—vision for the outside world as well as the inside church.

Leaders should be concerned to fulfill Christ's Great Commission, not simply maintain the status quo. Only as the church catches the vision of Christ's authority and power and senses the sovereign fullness of the gospel for the needs of the world will its own needs be met. God has designed the church's corporate worship and ministry within the body to provide a dynamic for outward ministry to the world. Such outgoing ministry will bring a return of blessing and renewal unavailable through any other means.

Exalting Christ and the authority of God's Word will deepen a church's quality of spiritual life, dignify the ministry, strengthen the bond of faith and motivate the service of disciples. Today's heresy that proclaims all truth to be relative erodes the authority of Christ and the Word. Disciples must be taught convictions based upon authoritative truth, not merely preferences based on subjective personal thought.

The Reformation church traditionally has confessed itself to be "a congregation of saints in which the Bible is rightly taught and the sacraments rightly administered." The Scots Confession of 1560 stated:[3]

> The notes of the true kirk of God, we believe, confess, and avow to be, first, the true preaching of the Word in which God has revealed himself to us, and secondly, the right administration of the sacraments which must be annexed to the Word and promise of God to seal and confirm the same in our hearts. Lastly, ecclesiastical discipline rightly administered as God's Word prescribes, whereby vice is repressed and virtue nourished.[4]

These early confessions may betray a somewhat limited vision of the nature and function of the church. But they stress what is foundational: leadership in the Word and holiness in fellowship. To lose sight of these central features is to lose sight of what is most significant to the church.

Sanctification: The Essential Grace

Proper discipleship will soon lead the growing new convert into sanctification. For the Thessalonian believers, the sanctifying grace of God produced in them both worshipful service and evangelistic dynamic. This was not incidental. Sanctification is basic to the life and health of the church. It carries with it a deeply significant reproductive quality.

Today, because of past associations with holiness teaching, some believers misconstrue sanctification as an unwarranted, unhealthy separation from the world. Although believers certainly are not *of* the world, they are *in* the world as light and salt (Matthew 5:13–14). God expects them to be an effective influence in society.

A church in which the members experience and demonstrate sanctification has had a dramatic reordering of any casual discipleship. Living unequivocally for Christ and His kingdom separates believers from a worldly, self-oriented lifestyle (Matthew 6:33; Romans 12:1–2).

Knowing Christ as Sanctifier produces faith in His sovereign sufficiency and brings the anointing of His Holy Spirit to dedicated living and service (Galatians 5:22–25; Philippians 3:7–11; Acts 1:8). Discipleship in living union with Christ Jesus becomes deep and rich. God opens the believer's spiritual eyes. He judges the believer's sin. He prompts willing obedience. The indwelling Christ begins a day-to-day process of transformation that can be as radical as conversion. Francis Schaeffer, the well-known Christian apologist, said:

> The central problem of our age is not liberalism or modernism, nor the old Roman Catholicism or the new Roman Catholicism, nor the threat of Communism, nor even the threat of rationalism and the monolithic consensus which surrounds us. All these are dangerous but not the primary threat. The real problem is this: the church of the Lord Jesus Christ, individually and corporately, tending to do the Lord's work in the power of the flesh rather than of the Spirit. The central problem is always in the midst of the people of God, not in the circumstances surrounding them.[5]

This central problem must be confronted with the message of sanctification. When the church believes in and proclaims Christ as Sanctifier, new converts, babes in Christ, even unspiritual church members will be challenged to grow. Every area of the church will be affected for good. The inflow of sanctifying grace and the outflow of sanctifying power interface to produce mature disciples who are evangelistic and missionary.

Sanctification's essential place in the total nature and function of the church is difficult to overstate. Sanctification impacts the inflow of God's grace from the church's central core all the way to the church's contacts with the outside world. Conversely, sanctification empowers the church in its outflow of ministry, as we will see in chapter 9. The accompanying diagram is a further development of the "spirals" in my book, *Sanctification: An Alliance Distinctive.*[6]

Growing Up in Christ

As the diagram indicates, the "Growing up in Christ"—what we can call the centripetal side of sanctification—has a discernible pattern of development. It may not be possible to identify every one of the stages in each adherent or member, and there may be some variation in the order, but in general this is how it happens. Briefly we will look at these eight stages of disciple development, beginning with the basic contact and moving upward on the scale.

Contact. Unregenerate people are contacted with the gospel largely because sanctified members of God's church live and work in the world. Jesus said, "You are the salt of the earth. . . . You are the light of the world" (Matthew 5:13–14). God's people are witnesses to unregenerate people. They bear testimony to the truth of the gospel. Through sanctifying grace, saints carry the fragrance of Christ. They are "a letter from Christ" (2 Corinthians 3:3), "known and read by everybody" (3:2).

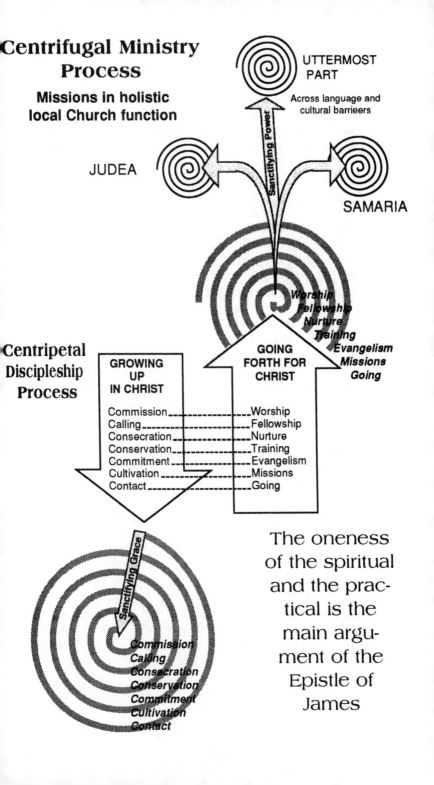

Centrifugal Ministry Process

Missions in holistic local Church function

UTTERMOST PART

Across language and cultural barrieers

JUDEA

SAMARIA

Sanctifying Power

Worship
Fellowship
Nurture
Training
Evangelism
Missions
Going

Centripetal Discipleship Process

GOING FORTH FOR CHRIST

GROWING UP IN CHRIST

Commission	Worship
Calling	Fellowship
Consecration	Nurture
Conservation	Training
Commitment	Evangelism
Cultivation	Missions
Contact	Going

Sanctifying Grace

Commission
Calling
Consecration
Conservation
Commitment
Cultivation
Contact

The oneness of the spiritual and the practical is the main argument of the Epistle of James

In the home, in the workplace, in community or recreational activity, in the school, in the marketplace, God's people are in contact with a needy world. Their awareness of peoples' needs and their ability to meet those needs develop as with their spiritual maturity.

Every church also has contacts in and through its services, activities, programs. Marriages and funerals produce contacts. Churches diligent in tracking all their contacts are surprised to discover that the contacts can exceed the number of church members. But the contacts only become true prospects when evangelism becomes a wellspring arising out of union with Christ and prayer becomes the believer's passion.

George Sweazey in *Effective Evangelism* has aptly observed that evangelism fails when it comes to be regarded as a special activity for special people at special times.[7] When new disciple-making is not the normal activity of the church, the church's life becomes superficial. The church by its very nature and function was designed to be a group of disciples reaching out into their communities in missionary action.

Cultivation. For a good harvest, ground must be cultivated properly and seed sown with discretion. Likewise for a spiritual harvest. It is God who makes things grow (1 Corinthians 3:7). Unripe fruit harvested too soon usually spoils. What is true in nature is also true in the spiritual realm. Healthy conversions occur when the unregenerate are vine-ripened. Seasoned disciple-makers will perceive the living Christ speaking through the Word by the Spirit to produce conviction of sin. They will not try to bring about repentance and faith by human ingenuity.

Friendly hospitality and openness that reach out in love are not contrived when Spirit-prompted. God works at both ends: in the person being reached and in the person reaching out. This is what makes personal evangelism so rewarding.

We dare not miss the fact that people continue to be saved within church buildings. The traditional Sunday evening gospel meetings may have lost their drawing power, but preaching for conversions should always characterize the church. Paul's comment about "an unbeliever or someone who does not understand" coming into the assembly (1 Corinthians 14:24–25) suggests that it will continue to happen. Even when the instruction is directed to believers, the Holy Spirit can use it to convict sinners.

When the apostolic ministry in the book of Acts is analyzed, it is clear that much evangelism took place when God's people were gathered. The presence of God in the midst of His people and the witness they have nobly borne through contact and cultivation will surely attract sinners to the church. Discipleship is best communicated in a group setting because it combines hearing with seeing. Sinners need to see discipleship demonstrated, and saints need to see sinners transformed. God who sanctifies believers and brings about their spiritual growth will also convict sinners and regenerate converts. Spiritual growth and conversion growth are produced by the same gospel and the same Spirit.

Commitment. Definite commitment and sound birth into the kingdom go together. Jesus said to Nicodemus, "I tell you the truth, no one can enter the kingdom of God unless he is born of water and the Spirit. Flesh gives birth to flesh, but the Spirit gives birth to spirit" (John 3:5–6). The generally accepted interpretation is that we need both a physical and a spiritual birth. This is certainly appropriate to the context: "You must be born again." But it is also possible that Jesus intended "water" to mean the Word, which is necessary to faith (Romans 10:9–10), just as the Spirit is necessary to life (Titus 3:5).

Unless faith is implanted by the Word and conviction is achieved by the Spirit, true repentance and the divine breath of life will not happen. The Spirit and the Word go together. What is subjective (spiritual life) also needs an objective base (the divine Word). A baby unable to take in sufficient oxygen is a blue baby. There are spiritual "blue babies," too.

True commitment is expressed in baptism, the outward sign of inward cleansing that has already taken place (1 Peter 3:21). This symbol of Christ's death, burial and resurrection identifies the believer as a follower of Christ. It is an initiatory rite, an ordinance of public confession, a testimony of intent both to the church and the world. It should be a prerequisite to church membership, signifying the believer's entry into the spiritual body of Christ.

Conservation. God's master strategy for making disciples is through properly functioning local churches. Converts need to take their places quickly as members of a local church where they can learn to walk with God and where accountability and responsibility are part of obedient discipleship. God's call to discipleship cannot be taken for granted by either the church or those who join its fellowship.

No one would think of joining a political party—or even a country club—without knowing something of its history and philosophy and the responsibilities it expects of members. Yet in the church, the most significant institution on earth, membership often is extended to people who have scant knowledge of its goals and objectives, its history, its beliefs, its organization and its leadership.

Conserving converts often succeeds or fails at this stage of discipleship. Knowledge of the church and its mission ought to inspire enthusiasm among new participants, just as lack of knowledge and vision may leave them unmotivated and listless.

The Lord's Table conserves fellowship with Christ and with the body of Christ. In the eucharist (literally "thank meal") believers are called to examine their commitment to Christ and the church (1 Corinthians 11:28). The Scriptures call the cup of blessing and the broken bread a "communion" (1 Corinthians 10:16). Participation, therefore, means that believers affirm their obedience to Christ and their love for the members of His body.

Thus conservation is more than the retention of converts in discipleship and church membership. It is also the retention of fresh, vital communion with God and with one another, energizing the whole church fellowship.

Consecration. All believers need to experience the sufficiency of Christ and the filling of the Holy Spirit. This comes in a consecration Christ performs when believers' identification with His death and resurrection becomes a union of life with Him. This union supplants the selfish, independent nature with which every one of us was born. It is a learning to rely on "Christ Jesus, who has become for us wisdom from God—that is, our righteousness, holiness and redemption" (1 Corinthians 1:30). It means staying attached to Christ (John 15:4).

Paul urged the disciples in Rome to "offer your bodies as living sacrifices, holy and pleasing to God" (Romans 12:1). He challenged them: "Do not conform any longer to the pattern of this world, but be transformed by the renewing of your mind. Then you will be able to test and approve what God's will is—his good, pleasing and perfect will" (12:2).

A transition of faith comes as we confront the cross and relinquish all of self to Christ. Old attitudes change; our lives are transformed with fresh newness. We have a progressive ability to discern God's will. In our yieldedness and dedication of life, we gladly recognize the Holy Spirit as a divine Person, sent to make Christ's indwelling real and to become our Comforter, Guide and Helper.

It is not by happenstance that members in the body of Christ "in all things grow up into him who is the Head" or become "joined and held together by every supporting ligament" (Ephesians 4:15–16). All members need to be persuaded that this is Christ's design for His church. All need specific instruction to make it happen.

Call. Much illusion and sentiment surround the biblical concept of *call*. As God summons believers to lives of fruitfulness, He frequently calls with specific direction. The Great Commission (Matthew 28:18–20) is a call that includes all believers. The Christian who witnesses at his or her in-town job may be fulfilling that call as effectively as someone else who is witnessing at an overseas missionary post. God calls us to be where and what He wants us to be.

God continues to invest Himself in believers. The leading of His Spirit, the opportunities of His providence and the graces and promises He provides through His Word are given for His people's personal involvement with Christ and His church. To the extent that God's people obey His purpose and will for them individually, they will bear fruit for Christ's kingdom.

As God's present-day disciples respond in obedience and "keep in step with the Spirit " (Galatians 5:25), God's call to them will be increasingly specific. The Scriptures speak about the "measure of faith " (Romans 12:3) believers possess as they relate to other members in the church. God's own gift or gifts are to be realized as fitting the good of the whole body under Christ's Headship (1 Corinthians 12:7). Christ places His followers in the body and fits their gifts into its function. The call of God by His Word and Spirit causes the discipleship process to operate with deepening effect.

Consecrated believers will be fruitful servants in their obedience to God's calling. All members of the body, men and women, are really ministers of Christ. As the discipleship process develops in sanctifying grace and power, the church will be characterized by enlarged faith and new horizons of vision.

Commission. In the providence of God, there are those whom God selects and gifts for specific leadership in the church. Paul mentions apostles, prophets, evangelists, pastors and teachers (Ephesians 4:11) as particular gifts to equip God's people for service. Normally, through the process of disciple-making in the church, God calls and gifts certain ones who enter vocational training to serve the church. As their calling and qualifications are confirmed, they are subsequently ordained and commissioned by the church.

Recruitment for such ministry should be a special concern for the church. The selection of His potential apostles was Jesus' first act as He began His ministry. He made His final selection only after a full night of prayer (Luke 6:12). Quality leadership flows from quality discipleship. The two go hand in hand. To lose the connection between discipleship and leadership is to lose the affirmation and confirmation necessary for continuity of strong leadership.

Too often churches expect Bible colleges and seminaries to independently produce pastors, missionaries and vocational Christian workers. From the biblical standpoint, these future church leaders must receive their calling from Christ *in the church*, where discipleship precedes leadership and where the corporate body recognizes the calling of God upon the disciple to larger leadership responsibility. Quality training for leadership can only be built on quality discipleship.

When discipleship does not include the calling of some to leadership ministry, the church has not reached responsible maturity. The wholeness of life, the mental integrity, the moral purity and the spiritual insight needed for church leadership come only through the steady, persevering discipleship that God has ordained for the church as a whole.

Only as the church meets its corporate responsibility to prayerfully choose and support its elders, deacons, deaconesses and other leaders, can we expect that church to live up to its potential. The selection of qualified leaders is the church's most serious and most blessed privilege. It promises the highest return and the greatest ministry benefit to the church.

The casual and irresponsible attitude of many local churches in regard to the training of leaders, whether in the church itself or in colleges and seminaries, is not short of tragic. Jesus made leadership training His priority when "he appointed twelve—designating them apostles—that they might be with him and that he might send them out to preach" (Mark 3:13–14). He foresaw that leadership training was the cutting edge of His church's future. He knew as well that to be "with him" was a primary necessity if He was to send them forth to preach in His name.

This "inworking"—being with Jesus—in the outworking of disciple-making are closely related. A person cannot be intimately related to the Lord without relating to His purpose and will. Conversely, trying to relate to the purpose and will of the Lord without relating to Him in identification and union is futile. Jesus warned, "Apart from me you can do nothing" (John 15:5).

God designed the church to relate the inworking of sanctifying grace to the outworking of sanctifying power in fruitfulness. The next chapter will discuss how the coupling of these two concepts results in Christ-honoring ministry.

Endnotes

[1]Arthur Matthews logically argues that the group must have been more extensive than just the 11 remaining disciples. Citing the comment, "But some doubted," (28:17), Matthews observes that all of the immediate disciples by then were firmly convinced that Jesus had risen from the dead. Therefore, it must have been a larger group to whom Jesus addressed His Great Commission. In fact, it could have been the "more than five hundred of the brothers" (1 Corinthians 15:6) referred to by Paul.

[2] Charles Colson with Ellen Santilli Vaughn, *The Body* (Dallas: Word Publishing, 1992), p. 282.

[3] "The Augsburg Confession of 1530" by Henry Beltenson, *Documents of the Christian Church* (London: Oxford University Press, 1947), p. 298.

[4] Ibid.

[5] Francis A. Schaeffer, *No Little People* (Downer's Grove: Intervarsity Press, 1974), p. 64.

[6] Samuel J. Stoesz, *Sanctification: An Alliance Distinctive* (Camp Hill, PA: Christian Publications, Inc., 1992), pp. 111, 114.

[7] George E. Sweazey, *Effective Evangelism* (New York: Harper & Brothers, 1953), p. 18.

6

The Ministry
of the Church

*T*he ministry of the church to its own membership and its ministry to others are not, from the viewpoint of the Scriptures, separate entities. Just as faith and deeds are interrelated (James 2:18, 26), so these two aspects of the church's work are interrelated. The gospel preached by Paul to the Thessalonians with power and deep conviction (1 Thessalonians 1:4) also "rang out" from the Thessalonians "in Macedonia and Achaia" and "everywhere" (1:8). Real faith always expresses itself in corresponding action. We expect nothing less from a God who always acts in character with intelligent purpose.

As we have seen, The Christian and Missionary Alliance from its earliest days believed that Jesus' Great Commission (Matthew 28:18–20) was to the church itself, not to a parachurch missions agency. The universality of Christ's authority, power and presence is to be expressed through His ordained body, the church. World evangelization is the function of the church.

Simpson called the early "branches" of the Alliance "irregular" because they supplemented the traditional church. The deeper life was their formational emphasis; missions was their functional emphasis. For Simpson, these elements of faith (deeper life belief) and deeds (missions) affected the entire structural nature and function of the church. They were foundational principles not adequately emphasized by other agencies or churches. He wrote:

> The great mistake of the church has been its failure to recognize God's plan in ultimate and full perspective. . . . The whole truth is necessary to rightly understand each part.
>
> The word "power" expresses the deep underlying truth that runs through the entire book of Acts. A supernatural Person has come to indwell the bosom of the church. While Jesus is at the throne as Head of the church, the power of the Holy Spirit is the heart of the church at work.[1]

It was this understanding of God's design for existing churches that motivated Simpson's actions. In establishing his "branches," Simpson certainly harbored no elitist or separatist motives. Rather, he saw from the Scriptures that the enthroned, sovereign Head of the church, in sending His Holy Spirit to the church, intended for the Spirit to impact the nature and function of the church.

The Lord of the Church's Ministry

The absolute, unconditional supremacy of Christ finds its best expression in and through the church. In Simpson's mind, the church too often has had a limited view of God's plan. "The fullness of Jesus' power available to the church will never be known except in connection with the world's evangelization," Simpson said.[2] In another passage, he expressed his concern in these terms:

> The [church] has a divine pattern. Just as the tabernacle of old was to be constructed strictly according to the pattern that was shown to Moses on the Mount, so the church of Christ has a divine plan and should be in every particular constructed accordingly. The failure to do this has been the cause of all the apostasies, declensions and mistakes of the past eighteen centuries. It is the reason why the heathen world is still lying in darkness and crying to God against the unfaithfulness of His people.[3]

In Simpson's view, during the preceding 18 centuries the church had largely failed to follow God's design both in its spiritual and organizational structure. Historically the Reformation church relegated missions to a place outside its local function, nor did it recognize that Christ had sufficient authority and power to fulfill the missionary mandate. As a consequence, the church had greatly limited Christ's universal authority and sovereign power in and through the church.

Christ's majesty and His authority must be central within the total ministry of the church. The scope of redemption is commensurate to mankind's fall and relates to all creation. Paul says, "We know that the whole creation has been groaning as in the pains of childbirth right up to the present time" (Romans 8:22). God has subjected all of creation to the hope of coming redemption through Jesus Christ. That Good News is to be preached in the whole world before the end will come. For that He has designated the church, His body, "the fullness of him who fills everything in every way" (Ephesians 1:23).[4]

The Lord Himself has a program of redemption for which His church is the ordained instrument. God designed the church with a scope and capacity through which Christ's authority, power and blessing are to be manifested. The church is commissioned with resources and gifts to fulfill its mission. Article II in the General Constitution of The Christian and Missionary Alliance expresses its commitment as a church "to the glorification of the Triune God through worship and world missions, stressing the fullness of Christ in personal experience, building the Church and preaching the Gospel to the ends of the earth."[5]

Paul declares that unity and spiritual maturity are the goals of functional discipleship (Ephesians 4:13, see 4:13–16). The full extent of Christ's exaltation—and the church's exaltation with Him as His bride—is beyond comprehension. The context of Ephesians 4:13, especially 4:10, suggests that Christ will "fill the whole universe." Already God has "placed all things under his feet" (1:22). And the redeemed church, His bride, *will be there with Him.*

Disciples: The Object of the Church's Ministry

The task of the church is disciple-making. As we have seen, this is far more than winning new converts to Christ. It includes the spiritual formation of those new converts: a maturing process in worshipful service that anchors the body-life of the church to the "pillar and ground of truth" (1 Timothy 3:15). Growth into union with Christ and fellow believers and the extension of Christ's universal kingdom become primary quests. "This," says Simpson, "is what the Master meant when He said, 'He that believeth on me, the works that I do shall he do also; and greater works than these shall he do; because I go unto my Father.' "[6]

110

Christ's authority and power within the ministry of the church are contingent upon Christ's supremacy within its body-life. The empowered church recognizes its responsibility to model spiritual maturity as it reproduces.

In 1987, the Alliance General Council adopted a program called "Churches Planting Churches." Its purpose was stated in these words:

> To create by God's help and for God's glory a fresh vision, a deeper commitment and a new thrust in every Alliance church. . . . To aggressively evangelize communities and disciple believers to be Spirit-filled, maturing, reproducing church members. . . . To encourage the participation of every Alliance church in the evangelization of ethnic minority people and the planting of churches cross-culturally.[7]

Here is the mission statement of the Alliance Division of Overseas Ministries:

> To plant churches ultimately committed to world evangelization among people groups who have not yet received an understandable presentation of the gospel and among whom there is no indigenous church effectively evangelizing those people; and
>
> To plant churches among peoples responsive to the gospel, regardless of their previous exposure to Christianity, with a view to equipping those churches to evangelize unreached peoples and to plant missionary churches among them.[8]

It is clear from the above statements that The Christian and Missionary Alliance believes that planting missionary churches locally and cross-culturally is God's design for world evangelization. Nevertheless, the nature and function of disciple-making in those plantings are basic to their becoming missionary churches. To bypass the dis-

cipleship process is to fail to produce missionary churches.

The Ministry of Disciple-Making

In chapter 5 we looked rather thoroughly at disciple-
making and the forces within the local church that create
a climate for personal spiritual growth among the
church's members. In this chapter we take a different
tack: How do those growing disciples further the local
church's ministry?

The faith and deeds tandem with which we introduced
this ministry chapter is essential to all stages of body-life
development. James sets forth the principle in these
words:

> *What good is it, my brothers, if a man claims to have
> faith but has no deeds? Can such faith save him? Suppose
> a brother or sister is without clothes and daily food. If one
> of you says to him, "Go, I wish you well; keep warm and
> well fed," but does nothing about his physical needs, what
> good is it? In the same way, faith by itself, if it is not ac-
> companied by action, is dead.*
>
> (James 2:14–17)

Faith in Christ's authority and sufficiency must also be
demonstrated in the functional ministry of the church.
Simpson observed: "The church is failing and coming
short in her work. She is not making the work of foreign
missions her chief business, as Christ meant it should be.
The apostles gave their best men to it, but the church
today is playing at it."[9]

Christ's presence in power and authority within the
church's body-life expands from center to circumference
in several "faith/deeds" components. To plant reproducing churches, faith and deeds must first be fed with truth
and clothed in active obedience. Growth in spiritual grace
causes growth in functional power as faith is expressed in
deed and under sound corporate leadership.

The cultivation of disciples from conversion to maturity in Christ represents an "in-working progression," described in chapter 5. But with this in-working growth of faith there is a concurrent "outworking progression" of faith in ministry. These faith/deeds components occur at various stages of the individual church member's development and likewise for the church corporately. We shall look at these aspects of the church's ministry.

Worship/Commission. The commitment of The Christian and Missionary Alliance "to the glorification of the Triune God through worship and world missions" may seem at first to be a peculiar confluence of ideas. But worship relates to missions by providing dimension and substance. Because the church is commissioned by Christ to a worldwide mission, it looks to God in worshipful dependence for all of its life. As Christ is formed in believers and developed in them to the full measure of their spiritual capacity, they will be holy and strong as a corporate church for the vital ministry God has called them to.

The New Testament Greek word for worship means also "to serve." States Warren Wiersbe, well-known pastor, writer and broadcaster, "Worship is at the center of everything that the church believes, practices and seeks to accomplish. It has forced me to evaluate my own spiritual life and the priorities that help to direct it."[10]

The climactic worship drama of Scripture is played out in Revelation 5:6–10. Christ Jesus appears as a "Lamb, looking as if it had been slain." Standing "in the center of the throne," He takes the sealed scroll "from the right hand of him who sat on the throne." As He does so, the "four living creatures and the twenty-four elders" bow before Him, take up their harps and begin to sing:

> *"You are worthy to take the scroll*
> *and to open its seals,*
> *because you were slain,*
> *and with your blood you purchased men*

> *for God*
> *from every tribe and language and people*
> *and nation.*
> *You have made them to be a kingdom and*
> *priests to serve our God,*
> *and they will reign on the earth."*

Note how the worship—the "*worth*ship"—of Jesus Christ is tied to redemption: "With your blood you purchased men for God." Note the scope of redemption: "From every tribe and language and people and nation." True worship puts the priority of God's kingdom—Christ's work of redemption for all creation—front and center. Where that priority is not center stage, true worship is dysfunctional and unfocused.

Worship of God in His majesty and greatness is the motivation of dedicated service. As Wiersbe observes, wonder, witness and warfare will then become the meaning and challenge of the church's worship.[11] The wonder of Christ's authority, power and presence within the church inspires and motivates service. God sends His prophets, His Son, His Spirit, His apostles, His evangelists, His pastors and teachers and His church as witnesses to establish His kingdom. The challenge of warfare in God's universal plan and purpose heightens anticipation for Christ's return with the promise of glorious and final victory.

Fellowship/Calling. Paul assures the Corinthians, "God, who has called you into fellowship with His Son Jesus Christ our Lord, is faithful" (1 Corinthians 1:9). The calling into fellowship and holiness (1:2) gives form and substance to the church's faithfulness because God is faithful. The vertical fellowship with God results in horizontal fellowship within the body. Such fellowship strengthens as it deepens.

We need not read far between the lines to realize that the 72 whom Jesus sent forth (Luke 10:1) were followers in fellowship with Him. As He sent them out to witness regarding His kingdom, Jesus commented on the few laborers for a plentiful harvest and asked them to pray about that deficit. Jesus taught them the evangelistic method they should use and the message they should preach. He assured them they spoke for Him: "He who listens to you listens to me; he who rejects you rejects me" (10:16).

After their assigned ministry was fulfilled, the 72 returned "with joy," and Jesus, likewise "full of joy through the Holy Spirit," exalted God the Father in prayer. Simpson viewed the 72 as "the pioneers of the mighty army who were to succeed them in the coming ages."[12]

Jesus called the 72 "little children" (10:21). He called his 12 disciples "friends" (John 15:15). He said to them, "You did not choose me, but I chose you and appointed you to go and bear fruit—fruit that will last" (15:16). Jesus also had an inner circle—Peter, James and John—(see Mark 5:37; Luke 9:28; Mark 14:33). Peter's practical activism and impetuosity, which often landed him in trouble, were offset by John's mysticism and sanguine personality. James seemingly provided a balance. Surely if the human Jesus needed this deeper fellowship and support, how much more His servants? There are inner strivings that only intimate fellowship can know and share.

This "funneling" effect of a deeper, closer fellowship demonstrates the need for concentrated sharing and mutual accountability. Christ's own promised presence where two or three are gathered in His name (Matthew 18:20) draws the larger fellowship to a center of gravity where intimacy in ministry brings earth into touch with heaven's highest interests. Strong fellowship in prayer, in sacrificial concern and in service is found only in faithful relationships honored by the presence of our Savior God. Spiritual fellowship transcends socializing and rises above personality traits. It relates God's calling through diverse gifts and finds enrichment and strength from others of like faith.

Paul had met Jesus on the road to Damascus (Acts 9:5), had been "caught up to paradise" and had "heard inexpressible things" (2 Corinthians 12:4). Yet in his ministry he seems always to need a partner, at times three or more, to support him in fellowship.

Circumstances do not determine fruitful ministry. Nor do natural gifts determine a person's call to service. Faith finds solid ground in firm discipleship, and God's call to service not infrequently comes amid spiritual fellowship. As believers offer themselves in spiritual worship and allow themselves the transformation of renewed minds (Romans 12:1–2), the collective body is able to test and approve God's good, pleasing, perfect will. It happened at Antioch (Acts 13:1–3); it happens still.

Nurture/Consecration. Spiritual nurture helps to bring about maturity. That nurture comes through a consecrated life. We have just looked at Romans 12:1–2. Paul is exhorting believers to a consecration crisis leading to mind renewal and to a disposition of worshipful service. But consecration also stimulates a process. As believers see the Lord through His Word and by His Spirit, they gradually are "transformed into His likeness with ever-increasing glory" (2 Corinthians 3:18). Spiritual nurture and consecration go hand in hand.

The reality of Christ as Sanctifier and the demonstration of a consecrated life will affect the church's fellowship and worship experience. Spiritual nurture will not produce maturity if the heart is full of selfish desire and the will has not been surrendered to God. But fellowship in prayer, in sacrificial service and giving that flows out of consecrated worship inevitably will challenge those new in the faith and those who have never entered into full partnership with Christ. There is something attractive and penetrating about Spirit-filled living.

In the transfiguration of Jesus, the glory of God from within transformed His very appearance. Wiersbe remarks:

> It is this kind of experience to which you and I are called by God. He wants to transform us. He also wants to work through us to transform the people and circumstances that make up our lives. Every Christian is either a "conformer" or a "transformer." We are either fashioning our lives by pressure from without, or we are transforming our lives by power from within. The difference is—worship.[13]

Worship that does not result in spiritual fellowship and nurture becomes a masquerade. Consecration must be nurtured. It is not experience-centered but Christ-centered. The church is a biblical "operating model" when it communicates Christ as Sanctifier. Ministry leaders who have a vision of the meaning of consecration will have deep concern for nurture. This concern will emanate from even the casual contacts in their leadership ministry. They will envision the church as being made one with Christ so that the motivation that ruled Him will rule them.

A vision of consecration will mean an intense narrowing of interests that are trivial and an immense broadening of interest in God's kingdom work. The church preoccupied with trivial pursuits is on a spiritual treadmill. New converts must be led to a sanctified and Spirit-filled life that results in worshipful service. We dare not settle for anything less. If the church is an "operating model," new believers will desire the fullness found in Christ. The whole church will move toward a broader and more effective ministry as consecration is nurtured.

In Paul's final appeal to the Corinthians he wrote: "Finally, brothers, good-by. Aim for perfection, listen to my appeal, be of one mind, live in peace. And the God of love and peace will be with you" (2 Corinthians 13:11).

The pursuit of excellence is a fruit of consecration and union with Christ and His body. The highest possible caliber of person is needed in leadership. Allowing unqualified members to carry out leadership functions simply because "everyone ought to have a chance" is not in the best interest of the church's nurture nor does it exalt "the God of love and peace."

Training/Conservation. Jesus in His Great Commission instructed the church to "make disciples, . . . teaching them to obey everything I have commanded you" (Matthew 28:19–20). A trained disciple will be a conserved disciple in responsible membership. In training disciples, the church brings the truth and authority of God's Word into practice for the building up of the church.

Jesus spoke about a farmer who went forth to sow seed for a harvest (Matthew 13:4–8). Some fell on the hard path and birds ate it. Some fell on rocky ground where there was insufficient soil to sustain it. Some fell where weeds choked its growth. Most of the seed (the wording used by Mark implies this idea) fell on good soil where it produced a harvest.

Certainly the farmer would not deliberately sow seed on a hardened path or among stones and thorns. It landed in those places unintentionally. The point of the parable is that the "sowing" of the gospel brings results *if those who receive it are prepared.*

The church has been remiss by not training spiritual agriculturalists. Too often the church has majored in random seed-sowing. It has given little attention to soil preparation and the nurture of the young plants that have resulted. Making fruitful disciples will lead to many more converts and will develop dynamic, effective leaders who will prepare God's people for works of service so that the body of Christ may be built up.

According to missiologist Peter Wagner, the church growth principles set forth by Donald McGavran had a clear objective: ". . . to make more effective the propagation of the gospel and the multiplication of churches on new ground. [McGavran] believed that the expenditure of $300 million a year out of North America for overseas missions could be made to yield much more Christianization."[14]

McGavran saw church growth in terms of multiplying churches overseas where independent missions agencies had usually failed in church planting. His principles have now been adapted to America. Unchurched or underchurched "new ground" has often been more fertile than old ground, but the neglect of old ground is questionable. It appears to pass judgment on God's unfinished work in older, established churches and communities.

The aim of the church is to reach more people for Christ and to lead those reached to become responsible and fruitful members. Too often, however, candidates for membership are not steered toward any kind of discipleship. They receive little or no practical training in godliness.

Training is also essential for a church's children and youth. If a church conserves its biological growth, it will generally increase not only numerically but also in spiritual depth and maturity. Teaching and training should begin in Christian homes, of course, but the church supplements that effort with essential indoctrination and practice.

Evangelism/Commitment. Biblical disciple-making is a cyclical process anchored in total commitment to Christ. That evangelism is a corporate endeavor supported by a deeper life message and by models of maturity becomes apparent as the doctrine of the church is better understood. Merely to make disciples without the benefit of a spiritual local church to further nurture them and employ their gifts is self-defeating.

As Samuel Wilson, Alliance missionary, researcher and writer, puts it, "The gospel in hermitage is near meaningless. The kind of living community that helps me discover the gospel's meaning is, according to Christ, the credential of the church to the world. . . . Only as churches are planted in a people group is there any possibility of producing a gospel movement capable of evangelizing."[15]

True evangelism anticipates total commitment, a commitment that should be modeled by the church. New converts do not immediately realize the cost of discipleship, though Christ's Lordship is unequivocal to their salvation. Becoming aware that their old nature is still with them and must be crucified volitionally in order for Christ's Lordship to triumph in their lives is part of discipleship. When and how this awareness comes is not the issue. Ideally it should take place as soon as possible. There are no uniform patterns of spiritual growth, but a Spirit-filled life is a settled one. Trying to stereotype holiness is to lose its creative vitality, but neglecting its necessity is to lose its reality.

Simpson believed that although baptism was initiatory, it looked forward to entire sanctification. By this he meant that converts were to anticipate an experiential identification with Christ through death to sin and self and the filling of the Holy Spirit.[16]

Baptism was commanded by Jesus; it is not an option. It is an overt rite and declaration of commitment—a commitment with definite experiential and progressive meaning.

The church fully committed to Christ will seek to develop strategies for evangelism that work best in its own cultural setting. Not all members will have the gift of evangelism, but all who are fully committed to Christ will participate in evangelism through intercession, through contacts and the cultivation of friends, by hospitality and by readiness to share the gospel. Corporate evangelism is basic to personal evangelism and for the development of the gift of evangelism.

Personal evangelism develops as church members contact and cultivate unsaved people in the local community and put them in touch with the Savior, Jesus Christ. But evangelism is most effective when it is a wellspring of worship, fellowship, nurture and training within the corporate body, a locus for sound conversions and lasting commitments.

Missions/Cultivation. Winning the lost to Jesus Christ has both a local and a global dimension. Evangelism that is only local in vision is neither tailored to fulfill Jesus' Great Commission nor equipped in faith with the authority, power and sufficiency that Christ promised (see Acts 1:8). Evangelism and missions complement each other in the dynamics of Christ's kingdom work.

Evangelism that is motivated only by a desire to see the local church grow numerically is deficient. The church, like the individual believer, must lose its life to find it. Christ will not be conformed to any church's selfish agenda. Evangelism at home must be motivated by a pure desire to bring lost people to the Savior who loves them and died for them.

The church needs to cultivate world evangelization—missions—as an accompaniment to evangelism. Missions is not an added obligation to evangelism but an integral part of the church's founding purpose. Missions moves up the timetable for the Lord's return and the coming of His kingdom. As we earlier noted, Isaiah exhorted Israel:

> *"Enlarge the place of your tent,*
> *stretch your tent curtains wide,*
> *do not hold back;*
> *lengthen your cords,*
> *strengthen your stakes.*
> *For you will spread out to the right and to the left;*
> *your descendants will dispossess nations*
> *and settle in their desolate cities.*
>
> *"Do not be afraid; you will not suffer shame.*
> *Do not fear disgrace; you will not*
> *be humiliated. . . .*

> *For your Maker is your husband—*
> *the LORD Almighty is his name—*
> *the Holy One of Israel is your Redeemer;*
> *he is called the God of all the earth."*
> (Isaiah 54:2–5)

This call of the prophet is amplified in the New Testament in Christ's Great Commission. The call is always to greater things:

> *Rise up, O men of God!*
> *Have done with lesser things;*
> *Give heart and soul and mind and strength*
> *to serve the King of kings.*[17]

Though the kingdom tarries long, the Lord will be no man's debtor! Therein lies the majestic nobility of the church.

Unless both missions and evangelism are pursued simultaneously with a focus on Christ's sovereign fullness, the church will be limited in its vision and purpose. For evangelism to thrive, it must be planned and promoted and its results intentionally conserved by the church. Everything the church does is for the purpose of advancing God's kingdom.

Going/Contact. Both evangelism and missions evolve from a lifestyle and mind-set developed in worship, fellowship, nurture, training and cultivation within the corporate church. But evangelism may be a very natural communication event.

In Jesus' Great Commission, the command, "Go and make disciples," reads literally, "As you go, make disciples." The only imperative is to make disciples. The "going" is simply a consistent walk with God, wherever the Christian is going, whether to a job, to the marketplace, to visit a friend. The early church knew nothing about programmed methods of evangelism.

Believers simply lived Christ-like lives in a pagan world and shared the Good News with their contacts. With natural freedom they told people what they knew and had experienced. Without doubt some of our canned and stilted efforts at evangelism would seem incongruous to a believer in first-century Jerusalem.

Contact for evangelism is an ordered consciousness that God is providentially at work, making His people witnesses of Christ's power to save. Any witness can give evidence concerning what he or she has personally experienced; it may take a disciple "to give the reason" (1 Peter 3:15) for the hope he or she has. The passively indifferent Christian will not have convincingly deep convictions about the person of Christ or the power of the Holy Spirit. The disciple engaged in a progressive walk with God should be able to express both in the daily "going" experiences of life.

The In-Working and Out-Working of Ministry

From the beginning, the deeper life and missions have characterized The Christian and Missionary Alliance. As we have already noted, this dual emphasis has been formational in the nature of the Alliance and its function. The validity and viability of this heritage may appear more relevant to members of a past interdenominational missionary society than to the church denomination that the Alliance has become. But the opposite is true. The organizational change has not invalidated the earlier convictions of the Alliance.

During his presidency, Louis L. King, sensing possible tension on this issue, made this assessment:

> The genius of the Alliance is its focus upon Christ Himself. The chief outgrowth of this centrality of Christ is not merely an organization with missionary activity. It is a missionary organization. Being fully rooted in Christ, it functions in full obedience to the Great Commission. These two aspects, expressed in

the phrases "Jesus Only" and "So Send I You," fuse into the distinctive characteristic of The Christian and Missionary Alliance. We need to deal with tensions regarding the priority of missions. . . . How shall we come to grips with this issue? What are to be our priorities? What is our reason for existing? How do we view the missionary mandate of The Christian and Missionary Alliance?

If the Alliance is to cope successfully with these and other questions, we must do so with flexibility and insights given of God. Methods and strategies may change, but God's directive does not. Often we are caught defending methods when we should be accenting principles.[18]

Ministry in its in-working is intimately related to ministry in its out-working. As Simpson strongly believed, *being* is more essential than *doing*. The church's spiritual nature is basic to its ministry. Each is necessary to the other. The church that takes a holistic view of its nature and function will express its faith by its works. "All missionary enterprise," Simpson said, "must have its source in deeper spiritual life."[19]

Jesus' Great Commission was intrinsic to the early church's ministry, but in the subsequent centuries this has seldom been true. The argument that only independent associations of church people can sustain missions translates to the conviction that the church itself cannot reproduce itself in cross-cultural ministry. But why not? Did it not do so in New Testament times?

The problem is that the church, instead of modeling a true missionary church, has been inclined to make missions an ad hoc ministry of church people. But the Great Commission belongs to the whole church, not simply to scattered individuals within it.

When Jesus Christ, the Head and Lord of the church, is allowed to work within the church in the lives of all of the church's members, the church will begin to work out this great salvation in evangelization, locally and to the ends of the earth.

Endnotes

[1] A.B. Simpson, *Christ in the Bible*, Vol. XVI, op. cit., p. 30.

[2] A.B. Simpson, *Missionary Messages*, op. cit., p. 18.

[3] Ibid., pp. 11–12.

[4] In *Sharpening the Focus of the Church* (Chicago: Moody Press, 1977), Gene Getz insightfully relates Scripture, history and culture to contemporary strategy in church function. In chapter 2, "Why the Church Exists," Getz cites Jesus' Great Commission (Matthew 28:18–20) as a primary text and identifies evangelism and edification as the main reasons for the church's existence. Getz makes an exhaustive list of texts in the New Testament under the two categories and seeks to demonstrate how this "focus" affects leadership, administration, organization and communication. He sees this, however, only in terms of building the local church and stresses the principle that every local body of believers must be responsible for its own community. He cautions against making foreign missions a substitute for local evangelism (p. 40). Nevertheless, he exhorts the church "to identify those who feel especially called by God to carry the good news in a special way out into the community and beyond the immediate community—even to 'the remotest part of the earth' " (p. 46).

Claiming to be giving readers a panoramic view of the church, Getz asserts, "Another area of obvious absolutes has to do with directives and objectives. The New Testament church consistently took the Great Commission seriously, both in the task of evangelism and edification" (p. 210). To Getz, evangelism and missions are evidently synonymous, and missions has no particular function within the local church except by ad hoc and incidental support of those who feel especially called to such work.

In contrast, the Alliance emphasis on the deeper life (Getz's edification) and missions (Getz's world evangelism) views the two as coordinating foci, the deeper life richer than mere edification and missions certainly much broader than world evangelism. The deeper life and missions are the intrinsic and extrinsic parameters of church life. Both impact significantly on church leadership, administration, organization and communication.

[5] Manual of The Christian and Missionary Alliance, 1989 edition, p. 3.

[6] A.B. Simpson, *The Holy Spirit, Power from on High*, Vol. II (Harrisburg, PA: Christian Publications, Inc., n.d.), p. 19.

[7] Division of Church Ministries statement prepared in April, 1988, and approved by the President's Cabinet and the Board of Managers.

[8] Alliance Division of Overseas Mission Statement, prepared in June, 1990, and approved by the President's Cabinet and the Board of Managers.

[9] A.B. Simpson, "Mission Work," supplement to *The Word, Work and World* (August, 1887), p. 106.

[10] Warren W. Wiersbe, *Real Worship* (Nashville: Oliver Nelson, 1986), p. 17.

[11] Ibid.

[12] Simpson, *Missionary Messages,* op. cit., p. 14.

[13] Wiersbe, op. cit., p. 31.

[14] C. Peter Wagner, *Your Church Can Grow* (Glendale: Gospel Light Publications, 1976), p. 13.

[15] Samuel Wilson, *MARC*, a publication of World Vision (March/April, 1983), p. 8.

[16] A.B. Simpson, "Baptism and the Baptism of the Holy Spirit," *The Christian and Missionary Alliance* (May 17, 1902), p. 286.

[17] William P. Merrill, 1867–1954.

[18] Louis L. King, "Pastoral Letter to the Church," (May 28, 1983,) p. 2.

[19] A.B. Simpson, "Aggressive Christianity," *The Christian and Missionary Alliance* (September 23, 1899), p. 260.

7

Service: The
Church's Occupation

*A*s the function of the church is best understood by discipleship, its nature is best described by servanthood. Isaiah's messianic image of the suffering Servant (interspersed in chapters 42–61) grows in significance as the New Testament unfolds.

Paul told the Philippian believers their attitude should match Christ's:

> *Who, being in very nature God,*
>   *did not consider equality with God something*
>   *to be grasped,*

> *but made himself nothing,*
>   *taking the very nature of a servant,*
>   *being made in human likeness.*
> *And being found in appearance as a man,*
>   *he humbled himself*
>   *and became obedient to death—*
>   *even death on a cross!*
>   (Philippians 2:5–8)

It is almost more than we can take in. The Sovereign of the Universe, the Creator of interstellar galaxies, the Designer of eyes and circulatory systems, the One who locked incredible power into the incredibly small atom— *He* humbled Himself. *He* took on humanity as a permanent form. *He* became obedient to death—and the cruelest of deaths besides. How many world rulers would take such a course, regardless of the worth of the cause? *Would we?*

Jesus' servant attitude, however incomprehensible from a human perspective, is fact—attested by the Holy Scriptures. And in His servanthood, Jesus modeled for His church an attitude, a mind-set that He expects His followers to apply personally and corporately.

As Paul penned his exhortation to the Philippians, he was not simply urging such an attitude on others. It was his own fixed disposition as well. Consistently he identifies himself as "a servant" of Jesus Christ. Freed from the fetters of sin, he consistently lived the life of a servant, a servant of Christ Jesus and a servant of the church he gave his adult life to propagate.

To live as divinely freed people is to live as servants of God. Peter admonishes God's elect, "Live as free men, but do not use your freedom as a cover-up for evil; live as servants of God" (1 Peter 2:16). For God's people to "live as free men" without using freedom as a cover-up for evil discloses the true identity of biblical servanthood.

Nor is servanthood about to end. In Revelation's final picture of believing saints, after the New Jerusalem has descended out of heaven, John gets this report: "No longer will there be any curse. The throne of God and of the Lamb will be in the city, and his servants will serve him" (Revelation 22:3). Servanthood and service never end. They will be our eternal joyous occupation.

The Nature of Servanthood

Servanthood is a divine attitude and disposition. Its intrinsic nature is divine in character. It does not come naturally to humankind's fallen nature. When believers exhibit a servant spirit, it is because they share the very life of Christ.

The church, as the body of Christ, expresses the life and mission of Christ in the world. Ever since Pentecost, the Holy Spirit embodies Christ within the church and inspires disciple-making through servanthood. Christ proclaimed the presence of the kingdom in His own Person when He announced, "The time has come. . . . The kingdom of God is near. Repent and believe the good news!" (Mark 1:15). But He did not come as a regal monarch. Rather, He fulfilled the prophecies of the Old Testament, particularly the suffering Servant image of Isaiah.

Jesus began His public ministry with an attitude and disposition that revealed His servant calling. John the Baptist considered himself unworthy to baptize Jesus. But Jesus told him it was necessary in order to "fulfill all righteousness" (Matthew 3:15). Jesus voluntarily submitted Himself to the obedience that baptism symbolized—obedience unto death in service for the world. As He "went up out of the water," the heavens opened and the Holy Spirit descended like a dove and lighted upon Jesus (3:16) and a Voice from heaven paraphrasing Isaiah 42:1 announced, "This is my Son, whom I love; with him I am well pleased" (3:17).

Some time thereafter, this new Galilean Prophet stood up in the synagogue at Nazareth and identified Himself to the people of His hometown by quoting Isaiah 61:1–2:

> *"The Spirit of the Lord is on me,*
> *because he has anointed me*
> *to preach good news to the poor.*
> *He has sent me to proclaim freedom for the prisoners*
> *and recovery of sight for the blind,*
> *to release the oppressed,*
> *to proclaim the year of the Lord's favor."*
> (Luke 4:18–19)

Jesus came to serve the needy, the poor, the imprisoned, the blind, the oppressed.

Similarly this motif of the suffering Savior emerges as His ministry of power and authority developed into confrontation with the Pharisees. Matthew sees it as the fulfillment of another text from Isaiah (42:1–4):

> *"Here is my servant whom I have chosen,*
> *the one I love, in whom I delight;*
> *I will put my Spirit on him,*
> *and he will proclaim justice to the nations.*
> *He will not quarrel or cry out;*
> *no one will hear his voice in the streets.*
> *A bruised reed he will not break,*
> *and a smoldering wick he will not snuff out,*
> *till he leads justice to victory.*
> *In his name the nations will put their hope."*
> (Matthew 12:18–21)

Father/Son: Jesus Models Servanthood

The meekness and humility Jesus evidenced in the midst of a hostile and sin-blinded world reveal His submissiveness to the Father. His humanity limited Him to a specific geographical land and a stubbornly rebellious and resistant people as He fulfilled His mission. Such limitations, the Scriptures observe, exposed Him to our trials: "We do not have a high priest who is unable to sympathize with our weaknesses, but we have one who has been tempted in every way, just as we are—yet was without sin" (Hebrews 4:15). The secret of His power and authority was His servant mind-set. He would manifest God the Father, at the same time serving people at their point of need.

Under that attitude and motive, Jesus' ministry prospered, and His present servant ministry of intercession will continue to prosper until some from every nation and tribe and tongue and people put their faith in Him. Isaiah speaks of the suffering Servant who will "bring forth justice" (Isaiah 42:3). Servanthood characterized not only Jesus' ministry on earth, but it continues to define His ministry through His disciples and the church.

Scholars have questioned whether the suffering Servant passages in Isaiah refer to Messiah or to Israel. The texts very clearly impose messianic qualities upon Israel as God's chosen servant. No doubt both may be implied because redeemed Israel is predestined to serve God, first through a faithful remnant and then through the church and its messianic Head. What the Old Testament portrays concerning Israel as God's chosen servant applies to the New Testament church as a result of Christ's atoning death on the cross. In anticipation of the church, Jesus prayed in Gethsemane:

> "My prayer is not for [my disciples] alone. I pray also for those who will believe in me through their message, that all of them may be one, Father, just as you are in me and I am in you. May they also be in us so that the world may believe that you have sent me."
>
> (John 17:20–21)

Jesus submitted fully to the Father and gave Him total obedience. Between them there was unity of spirit to serve the needs of the world. This same relationship is to characterize Jesus' disciples. As Jesus' effectiveness was dependent on His servant nature, so also is the effectiveness of the church. As the church succeeds in servanthood,

Satan's opposition will rise. To build his unrighteous kingdom, he will arrogantly attempt to interdict the authority Christ intends His disciples to share with Him in servanthood. He does so by projecting himself as the god of this world and by appealing to our selfish desires. In fact, he comes "to steal and kill and destroy" (John 10:10).

A Hard-to-Express Concept

Jesus claimed no special reputation as Son of Man, yet He came to give believers authority over Satan and all his wiles, to provide right of access to the Father in prayer, to grant to His followers the privilege of being coheirs with Him in His kingdom. Jesus claimed great drawing power: "I, when I am lifted up from the earth, will draw all men to myself" (John 12:32). But this drawing power of Jesus would be through the church and the church's oneness with Him. This attraction to Jesus is not to be, and cannot be, dammed up for self-enjoyment. Jesus said, "Whoever believes in me, as the Scripture has said, streams of living water will flow from within him" (John 7:38). He foresaw the church—those who believed in Him—in corporate service.

The biblical concept of servanthood is difficult to express in English. It is not the typical slave-master relationship. Mosaic Law made provision for an indentured Israelite, eligible for freedom after six years, to opt to continue to serve his master (Exodus 21:6; Deuteronomy 15:17). Perhaps the master had been especially good to him, perhaps the master had given him a wife who in turn had given him children. Rather than to walk away from these benefits, he could opt for *voluntary* servitude. From then on he served his master not from obligation but from love. He voluntarily relinquished his own rights and prerogatives in order to carry out the purposes and will of his master.

Jesus' ministry fully exemplified such servanthood. To please His Father God, He willingly set aside His heavenly identity, independence and self-determination. He accepted the limitations of humanity. He carried out His Father's purposes as though they were His very own. At last this Author of Life even submitted to *death*—a most cruel and shameful death, at that.

The Calvary heart of Jesus marks the Spirit-filled believer. Jesus' death was not that of a martyr, as people so frequently conceive it, but a substitutionary death. His servant spirit, manifested on earth and supremely on Mount Calvary, is vicariously reproduced by the Holy Spirit in the body-life of His church.

This servant attitude produces in the church the centripetal and centrifugal disciple-making relationships. It expresses itself first in our heart relationship to Christ. It then expresses itself in our outward relationship with other members of Christ's body, the church. The ultimate result of this dual relationship is a church that ministers to the whole world. To "grow up into" Christ (Ephesians 4:15) is to serve as Christ served and to extend the gospel of hope in Christ Jesus to all nations. Servanthood is a corporate spirit as well as an individual spirit. It is an infectious spirit of grace and love, one that so permeates the church's body-life that the world inevitably recognizes it and is attracted to it.

Evangelism and missions are not essentially methods or strategies, even though methods and strategies are necessary. Evangelism and missions are the result of a servanthood character and disposition. The nine-fold fruit of the Spirit—"love, joy, peace, patience, kindness, goodness, faithfulness, gentleness and self-control" (Galatians 5:22-23)—represents the character of Christ. When we "live by the Spirit" (5:25), we are manifesting Christ's character and disposition.

Servanthood and the Church's Mission

At the beginning of the 20th century, A.B. Simpson analyzed the evangelical church in America and concluded its pressing need was to become a deeper life community with a world mission. This ideal is depicted in the suffering Servant passages of Isaiah where messianic servanthood characterizes a people whose ultimate mission is to reach the nations. The kingdom message preached by Jesus and His apostles was implicitly a missionary message. Sin had blighted all of Creation. It groaned "as in the pains of childbirth" (Romans 8:22) awaiting the promised redemption. The Creator-God who through His Son's incarnation gave us Jesus Christ is the Redeemer-God who through His immediate family, the church, is establishing a kingdom that will reconcile earth and heaven. This is the reason Jesus could say, "This gospel of the kingdom will be preached in the whole world as a testimony to all nations, and then the end will come" (Matthew 24:14).

When we focus our attention on the servant nature of the church rather than on its organizational structure, we find a captivating image emerging. As we have noted, Isaiah's description of Christ as the suffering Servant is a prophetical description of Christ's body, the church, in the New Testament. From Isaiah's words we can clearly recognize the task of the church as a "suffering servant" community. Consider again Isaiah 42:1–4:

> "Here is my servant, whom I uphold,
>   my chosen one in whom I delight;
> I will put my Spirit on him
>   and he will bring justice to the nations.
> He will not shout or cry out,
>   or raise his voice in the streets.
> A bruised reed he will not break,
>   and a smoldering wick he will not snuff out.
> In faithfulness he will bring forth justice;
>   he will not falter or be discouraged
> till he establishes justice on earth.
>   In his law the islands will put their hope."

Through the New Covenant, the Lord God has bonded with a servant people who are called in righteousness to become a light for the Gentiles. Justice will be established on earth because the Creator-God is also the Redeemer-God. God the Lord will take hold of the hand of this servanthood community, and it will extend the light of divine knowledge until God's purpose is accomplished for the whole earth.

When threatened by persecution and even death, the early church went to prayer. In their prayer they recognized God in His majesty as Creator-Redeemer, and they recognized the role of Jesus as God's "holy Servant." In fact, for the church *servant* had taken on a bold new universal dimension. Notice their frequent use of the word as they prayed:

> *Sovereign Lord, . . . you made the heaven and the earth and the sea, and everything in them. You spoke by the Holy Spirit through the mouth of your servant, our father David:*
>
>> *"Why do the nations rage*
>>   *and the peoples plot in vain?*
>> *The kings of the earth take their stand*
>>   *and the rulers gather together*
>> *against the Lord*
>>   *and against his Anointed One."*
>
> *Indeed Herod and Pontius Pilate met together with the Gentiles and the people of Israel in this city to conspire against your holy servant Jesus, whom you anointed. They did what your power and will had decided beforehand should happen. Now, Lord, consider their threats and enable your servants to speak your word with great boldness. Stretch out your hand to heal and perform miraculous signs and wonders through the name of your holy servant Jesus.*
>
> (Acts 4:24–30)

The servant mind-set of the early church in this brief prayer unfolds forcefully. Four times they use the word *servant*. Twice they speak of the "holy servant Jesus."[1] They recognize the servanthood of David, and they identify themselves as servants in direct relation to the sovereign and universal Lord Jesus who is both Creator and Redeemer. The overmastering majesty of Christ's personal power captured these believers in servanthood.

"All One Body We"

Another suffering Servant passage, Isaiah 49:1–6, calls nations afar to recognize the nature of the Servant revealed in Israel. Notice again the frequent use of the word *servant*. Notice, too, the universal majesty and glory of Christ which God's servant people are to share:

> *Listen to me, you islands;*
> *hear this, you distant nations:*
> *Before I was born the LORD called me;*
> *from my birth he has made mention of*
> *my name.*
> *He made my mouth like a sharpened sword,*
> *in the shadow of his hand he hid me;*
> *he made me into a polished arrow*
> *and concealed me in his quiver.*
> *He said to me, "You are my servant,*
> *Israel, in whom I will display my splendor."*
> *But I said, "I have labored to no purpose;*
> *I have spent my strength in vain and for*
> *nothing.*
> *Yet what is due me is in the LORD's hand,*
> *and my reward is with my God."*
>
> *And now the LORD says—*
> *he who formed me in the womb to be his*
> *servant*
> *to bring Jacob back to him*
> *and gather Israel to himself,*

> *for I am honored in the eyes of the LORD*
> *and my God has been my strength—*
> *he says:*
> *"It is too small a thing for you to be my servant*
> *to restore the tribes of Jacob*
> *and bring back those of Israel I have kept.*
> *I will also make you a light for the Gentiles,*
> *that you may bring my salvation to the ends*
> *of the earth."*

God's redemptive plan goes far beyond restoring the tribes of Jacob. It encompasses every part of the universe that sin has blighted. The church's servanthood is not restricted to its own community, drawing people in; its mission is to the nations. God wants the power and authority of Jesus to be displayed through the church worldwide. Are times hard? Has the church seemingly spent its strength in vain? Are its members discouraged? The suffering Servant did not find it easy. He will reward those who persevere. His "Well done!" awaits the church's faithful service. "When he appears, we shall be like him" (1 John 3:2).

The way the church views itself is very important. Unless its commitment to Christ runs deep, unless its trust in God's promise for ministry is true to the nature of Christ, it will find its strength and potential sapped by discouragement and debilitating weakness. The church exists more for the benefit of an unreached world than for those who are already safely inside its sanctuary. Indeed, only as it saves the world God loves can it save itself.

The call of the gospel is not only to trust Christ for salvation but to fulfill a destiny of servanthood to a lost world. Through the sanctifying power of the Holy Spirit, whom the Father sent, the church is to magnify Christ Jesus its Lord. Servanthood is a stance of faith that will not always be vindicated by circumstances. But in the final judgment, the wisdom of service will be evident. Indeed it is so: "I am honored in the eyes of the LORD / and my God has been my strength" (Isaiah 49:5).

God wants His church to relate to Him personally, intimately. This kind of spiritual reality is not developed in the hermitage. It is cultivated and sustained by community relationships and the Spirit's anointing. The Spirit ministers to us not for the sake of private edification or ecstatic sensation but for the blessing of the community of believers in their service to the world.

The Scriptures hold out no prospect of relating to the Lord without relating as well to His community of believers called as a part of His purpose. The community is the gathering of Jesus' followers who together bear the same anointing as the early church: "With great power the apostles continued to testify to the resurrection of the Lord Jesus, and much grace was upon them all" (Acts 4:33).

Throughout, the Scriptures express balance between the corporate body of believers and the particular member, between the unity of the body and the uniqueness of each individual in it. The expression of diverse gifts must not be sacrificed to uniformity; neither should unity be threatened by the individual. Spiritual gifts are to enrich the fellowship and facilitate the church's service of extending God's glory locally and worldwide.

Servanthood and the Authority of Christ

The servant disposition and the authority of Christ go hand in hand. After Jesus laid down His life at Calvary, He arose from the dead and ascended to heaven. Enthroned at the right hand of the Father, He sent the Holy Spirit to indwell His disciples with His own servant attitude and with the authority He won for them on the cross.

The intense focus on the individual, so prevalent in our culture, does not fit the prophetically revealed image of the church. A church reflecting Calvary love is ready to sacrifice life itself for the sake of others (1 John 3:16). This posture of serving to the death matches the biblical pattern. Through the centuries it has enabled the church to fulfill with holy boldness God's universal purpose for it.

Jesus Christ, through the miracle of incarnation, identified with humankind in order to invest His power and grace of spirit in believers personally and the church corporately. The mission of the church is to make disciples, by baptizing, by teaching. The teaching curriculum is everything that Jesus commanded His disciples. The goal of the church is to grow up into Christ-like servanthood. The church submits to Him as He submitted to His Father God. Discipleship is reciprocal; it results in the church's corporate effectiveness. As the Word is proclaimed and taught, believers are confronted with new truth. They learn from each other and are affirmed. They are edified by each other's gifts and callings. The church appoints and elects members to different ministries matching their qualifications: pastors, teachers, evangelists, elders, deacons, deaconesses, worship leaders, counselors, Christian education superintendents, ushers. Whatever the office, its holders recognize themselves as accountable servants and models of discipleship. In a smoothly functioning church body the power and authority of Christ can be seen.

Too often we confuse special talents with spiritual gifts and appoint and elect to office on that basis. There *is* a difference. Every Spirit-filled member of the body has some gift in need of exercise. It may be as ordinary as faithful attendance, but that is important. It could be intercession, hospitality, the giving of money, encouragement, service to the elderly, working in the church nursery, visiting the sick, comforting those who mourn. The list of ministries that can build up the church is almost infinite.

Some servants are relieved of other responsibilities in order to serve the church full-time in leadership. Leaders help other gifted members to minister more effectively. They give balance and guidance to all areas of the church.

They express the church's servant role far beyond the walls of the meeting place.

Characteristics of Servanthood

True servanthood manifests itself in weakness: "When I am weak," declares Paul, "then am I strong" (2 Corinthians 12:10). The indwelling Holy Spirit, ministering the resurrection life of Christ Jesus, empowers the corporate body of believers to transcend human limitations.

Servanthood defers to others: "Be devoted to one another in brotherly love. Honor one another above yourselves" (Romans 12:10). Servanthood accepts others: "Let us stop passing judgment on one another. Instead, make up your mind not to put any stumbling block or obstacle in your brother's way" (Romans 14:13). Servanthood builds support for those weak in faith: "We who are strong ought to bear with the failings of the weak. . . . Each of us should please his neighbor for his good, to build him up" (Romans 15:1–2). Servanthood goes out of its way to cultivate unity: "Let us . . . make every effort to do what leads to peace and to mutual edification" (Romans 14:19). Do not suppose such manifestations of the power and authority of Christ will go unnoticed by the watching world.

Servanthood not only is displayed in the body but also in the world of people who need Christ. Servant disciples choose the front lines of battle, even by demonstrating the gospel in social action. Demonstration strengthens proclamation. David E. Schroeder, president of Nyack (New York) College, has expressed this well:

> The early church, with its Jewish cultural background, was not nearly as individualistic as Christianity is today. Because the Christian life was experienced corporately, almost communally, the church became an alternate culture that was a showcase for the values of the kingdom of God. There was no need for superstar evangelists or fanatical zealots.

The testimony of a community of disciples of Jesus Christ living in harmony, worshiping in reverential awe, ministering with compassionate love and courageously embracing their enemies was enough power to convince a skeptical world of the reality of Christian truth. Evangelism in those days was a by-product of a church that lived what it believed. There were no evangelism committees, no film series, no special seminars or crusades, not even any pocket-size booklets for personalized soul winning. Not that these things are not useful, but when they become substitutes for the community kingdom-living to which the church is called, they are concessions to failure.[2]

When it comes to people in need, the compassion of Christianity does not willingly discriminate between the regenerate and the unregenerate. Christ's love calls Christians to bear others' burdens and to compassionately demonstrate the gospel even to those who are enemies of the cross. Deeds of mercy may be catalysts for the gospel (although not substitutes for forthright gospel witness). Simpson writes, "Our acts of love and help may be [God's] links in bringing [people with temporal needs] to see the attraction of His love and listen to the gospel of His grace."[3]

At the turn of the last century, the New York Gospel Tabernacle was very active in social ministry. It sponsored rescue missions in the ghettos, homes for so-called fallen women, hostels for working girls and women living in the city, rest homes for the sick, orphanages, schools for deprived minorities. All of these were expressions of the servant-love of the church. They were demonstrations of the gospel and of kingdom living. But always Simpson accorded priority to evangelism and missions. Today, government subsidies and social welfare programs not withstanding, there still is room for the church to show its compassion and to demonstrate the gospel of Jesus Christ.

Servanthood in Body-Life

Strong continuity links the Old Testament and the New and ties the messianic servanthood of Israel to Christ and His church. But not transparently. Although the early church accepted the Old Testament as the Word of God, only gradually did its leaders and members realize from the prophecies that the gospel was for Gentiles, too, and that Christ intended for His church to have the major role in its propagation.

To fully understand the universality of the gospel, those first century believers needed the added revelation of the Gospels and the Letters—and ultimately the Acts and the Apocalypse. Meantime, through circumstances and divinely-timed events, Jesus was directing His church.

Jesus laid the church's foundation by forming a messianic community comprised of 12 disciples. To them he foretold the erection of its superstructure on the "rock" of faith in His messiahship and promised them that "the gates of Hades will not overcome it" (Matthew 16:18). Probably never have 12 men had greater responsibility thrust upon them.

Jesus taught that entrance into this new community required humility and childlike faith (Matthew 18:1–4). There could be no place in it for domineering and self-exalting people. It would be a disciplined community (Matthew 18:8–9, 15–17). Neither would this new community tolerate deceivers and liars—as Ananias and Sapphira demonstrated in their death (Acts 5:1–11).

Baptism, the initiatory rite of conversion, confronts the new believer's obedience and intentions very early. Simpson believed that baptism should be entered into with that understanding: "The ordinance of baptism, while initiatory of the Christian church, looks forward to entire sanctification and reaches its full significance only in complete death with Jesus Christ to self and sin."[4]

Following baptism, training and nurture should lead the convert to a submissiveness akin to Christ's—one that reaches out in faith to live in union with Him. Believers are to take up their cross and follow Jesus (Mark 8:34). If the church is to exercise power and authority in its servanthood, the provisions of salvation, received in conversion, must be laid hold of in sanctification.

With this understanding, Paul wrote: "The body is a unit, though it is made up of many parts; and though all its parts are many, they form one body. So it is with Christ. For we were all baptized by one Spirit into one body" (1 Corinthians 12:12–13).

For new converts, church membership demands an assimilation process that is critical. For new members to be offended and turned aside from obediently following Christ is a tragedy. On the other hand, receiving as a member in the fellowship a person who is not obedient to Christ's authority undermines the church and damages its witness.

Authority and Service

The "mystery" of the church (Romans 11:25; Ephesians 3:1–12) was specially revealed to Paul. It so captured his vision and motivated his spirit that, next to Jesus Christ, he became the most influential model of servanthood in the history of the church. His parish included Syrian Antioch, Asia Minor, the Asian archipelago, Greece, Rome—and possibly Spain. Although his first love was church planting in regions where the gospel was not known, his major investment in service to Christ was in the growth, nurture and guidance of these young churches. Paul considered it absolutely essential that both Jews and Gentiles should become heirs and sharers of the grace of life (Ephesians 2:14–22), united in the fullness of Christ and the gospel.

Paul considered himself "the worst" of sinners (1 Timothy 1:15) because he had persecuted the church of Jesus Christ (1 Corinthians 15:9). His faith in Christ and the church went deep. Whatever the misunderstandings of his motives, the misinterpretations of his teachings or

143

the problems in the churches, he never gave up on the church. He says, "I face daily the pressure of my concern for all the churches" (2 Corinthians 11:28). Paul never faltered in serving the church at its point of need.

Servanthood in the church is always patterned after Christ. Christ's effective service was a direct outcome of His submission to the Father and His union with Him. This He taught and modeled by fulfilling His servant role (Matthew 23:8–12; Mark 10:35–45; John 13:1–17). As Messiah, Jesus suffered vicariously for humankind's sin—something neither Israel nor the church is qualified to do—or needs to do. But the servanthood Jesus modeled in His character and mission the church can and does demonstrate through the saving and sanctifying power of Christ through the Holy Spirit.

The cross believers "take up" (Matthew 16:24) and the "yoke" they take on (Matthew 11:29) can be borne with much blessing because of Jesus' immediate presence and provision. His presence and provision indeed produce the qualities of life that provide the believer with fulfillment: rest, joy and peace.

The prominence of servanthood in the New Testament finds its acme in the church that represents Jesus Christ. "You know," Jesus said to His disciples, "that the rulers of the Gentiles lord it over them, and their high officials exercise authority over them. Not so with you. Instead, whoever wants to become great among you must be your servant, and whoever wants to be first must be your slave—just as the Son of Man did not come to be served, but to serve, and to give his life as a ransom for many" (Matthew 20:25–28). Jesus also said, "Whoever serves me must follow me; and where I am, my servant also will be. My Father will honor the one who serves me" (John 12:26).

The early church caught the infectious servant spirit of Jesus in local body-life by extending it through evangelism and missions. Alliance missionary Fred H. Smith has observed that the church has been given a prophetic and missionary role as a forerunner of the kingdom Christ came to establish. Its prophetic role, however, is not only proclamation of a message but the communication of its essence. "Without the Holy Spirit," Smith says, "the church would cease to be an instrument and sign of the kingdom of God in this world. It would soon revert to just another 'good institution' without being a 'holy institution.' "[5]

Qualifying the church for servanthood that is both prophetic and missionary depends heavily on a leadership that lives and teaches servanthood. Both the mission and the method of the church rely largely on leaders whose vision and life-style, in the words of Paul (Ephesians 4:12), "prepare God's people for works of service."

Endnotes

[1]The Greek word for "servant" in the two references to "your holy servant Jesus" is *pais*, translated "child" in the King James Version. Scholars claim the term has its roots in the servant passages of Isaiah. It suggests a majestic humility—that of a child being anointed as king, particularly when used in relation to "God's servant David." Strong cites also its translation as *servant* (especially a *minister* to a king; and by eminence to God)."

[2]David Eldon Schroeder, *Follow Me* (Grand Rapids: Baker Book House, 1992), pp. 131–132.

[3]A.B. Simpson, *Practical Christianity* (New York: Christian Alliance Publishing Co., 1901), p. 80.

[4]A.B. Simpson, *Baptism and the Baptism of the Holy Spirit*, op. cit., p. 286.

[5]Fred H. Smith, *Measuring Quality Church Growth* (unpublished thesis, Fuller Theological Seminary, April 1985), p. 92 in context of 83–96.

8

The Church's
Healing Ministry

*I*n a sweeping vision of the coming day of the Lord, Malachi four times predicts the whole Christian era as weighted with justice and judgment. But at the close of his relatively brief prophecy, he quotes God in these words: "But for you who revere my name, the sun of righteousness will rise with healing in its wings. And you will go out and leap like calves released from the stall" (Malachi 4:2). It is one of God's great, glorious promises.

Divine healing is portrayed in the Scriptures as neither exclusively physical nor exclusively spiritual. There is an important connection between the spiritual process that

147

precedes divine healing and the physical healing that follows, even when the latter is mysteriously hidden. The apostle Paul three times pleaded with the Lord to remove a physical malady troubling him. He called it "a messenger of Satan," (2 Corinthians 12:7). God refused to honor Paul's request. God had a purpose in the "thorn," as Paul subsequently realized. It was to keep him "from becoming conceited because of [the] surpassingly great revelations" God had shown him. Although in that instance Paul was not himself healed, the apostle often, in conjunction with his preaching and church founding, exercised a healing ministry to others.

To know Christ as Savior, Sanctifier, Healer and Coming King is simply to believe in His abounding fullness for redemption, including His power to heal to the full extent of humankind's fall. Redemption includes physical healing, but for this God may call us to await the "day he comes to be glorified in his holy people and to be marveled at among all those who have believed" (2 Thessalonians 1:10). Physical healing is not restricted to human understanding. Paul comments elsewhere, "How unsearchable [God's] judgments, / and his paths beyond tracing out!" (Romans 11:33).

Healing Terminally Ill Souls

The church is meant to be a caring community for spiritually lost and dying people. Evangelicals, with some encouragement from the Scriptures, have tended rather habitually to use the word *souls* as a substitute for *people.* In the Scriptures, the soul is described as the nexus—the center connector—of body and spirit: "spirit, soul and body" (1 Thessalonians 5:23). Soul is generally associated with the mysterious integration of life called personality and its animating force. Sin has resulted in a "living death" that afflicts the whole human race and the whole person: body, soul and spirit.

Evangelization locally and worldwide is the sine qua non of the church, its reason for existence. The church is to be engaged in a ministry to acquaint people with the love and care of the Lord Himself who is "not wanting anyone to perish, but everyone to come to repentance" (2 Peter 3:9). Jesus said He came that those who believed in Him might "have life, and have it to the full" (John 10:10).

In medieval times an order of charitable volunteers created hospices to minister to the terminally ill. These hospices were designed particularly for the under-privileged and the poor. The first hospitals were charitable institutions. The physicians who worked in these hospitals considered themselves ministers of mercy to the helpless and destitute. Today health care is big business—so gargantuan that it absorbs 14 percent of the American gross national income, so costly that it is beyond the reach of many.

Paul speaks of a day when "the creation itself will be liberated from its bondage to decay" (Romans 8:21). He says "the whole creation has been groaning as in the pains of childbirth right up to the present time" (8:22). It is a creation desperately needing the healing ministry of the church.

But the church is in danger of following the health care industry. It seems bent on becoming an institutional success at the expense of its servanthood calling. To feign love and care for the lost and dying in order to gain status and prestige is a cruel hoax. The church's Lord came as a Servant to seek and to save those who are lost. The church has a commission to take the Good News of Jesus to people who are terminally ill, to people who need to be saved for time and eternity.

The kingdom is for the brokenhearted and the poor in spirit (Matthew 5:3). Jesus came to "preach good news to the poor", to "proclaim freedom for the prisoners / and recovery of sight for the blind, / to release the oppressed, / to proclaim the year of the Lord's favor" (Luke 4:18–19). Many are blind to their need, but in their frustration they sense guilt. They are sorely oppressed by the devil. They have no consciousness of their opportunity to receive the Lord's favor.

Outside of Christ, No Salvation

The church that cares for people is aware that those outside Christ Jesus are eternally lost. The church is available to minister to people's needs and to share with them the gospel. When Jesus is lifted up through caring ministry, unbelievers will be moved to ask regarding the hope believers have (1 Peter 3:15). This, also, is a healing ministry that represents Jesus Christ and God's servant church.

The greatest gifts the church possesses are faith, hope and love, but the greatest of these is love (1 Corinthians 13:13). Without these gifts the methodologies and techniques devised by human wisdom become meaningless. The healing virtues of faith, hope and love are basic to evangelism.

The church is at risk of losing its heaven-born image. Unless it portrays a genuine spirit of loving care, its message may be in the tongues of men and of angels, but it will be but "a resounding gong or a clanging cymbal" (1 Corinthians 13:1).

The church's primary calling is to a servanthood that represents Jesus, who came to seek and to save what was lost. Isaiah perceived the passion of the suffering Servant when he wrote of Israel:

> *Ah, sinful nation,*
> *a people loaded with guilt,*
> *a brood of evildoers,*
> *children given to corruption!*
> *They have forsaken the LORD;*
> *they have spurned the Holy One of Israel*
> *and turned their backs on him.*
>
> *Why should you be beaten anymore?*
> *Why do you persist in rebellion?*
> *Your whole head is injured,*

your whole heart afflicted.
From the sole of your foot to the top of your head
  there is no soundness—
only wounds and welts
  and open sores,
not cleansed or bandaged
  or soothed with oil.
                                        (Isaiah 1:4–6)

Isaiah was not unaware of his people's sin, their enormous guilt and evil-doing, their rebellious stubbornness. But he was also acutely aware of the beatings his people had received, the injuries of mind and spirit they had borne. He was sensitive to his people's debility. Isaiah felt for his people. He was moved with compassion for Israel.

Jeremiah likewise empathizes with Israel's condition. He laments:

Since my people are crushed, I am crushed;
  I mourn, and horror grips me.
Is there no balm in Gilead?
  Is there no physician there?
Why then is there no healing
  for the wounds of my people?
                                        (Jeremiah 8:21–22)

The Church Offers What Hurting People Need

In contrast to the inane glamor and glitz and the hollow laughter by which sin entices its victims, the reality and beauty of Jesus Christ stands out in bold relief. Malachi, as we have noted, predicted as much: "The sun of righteousness will rise with healing in its wings."

Paul exhorts the Colossians to "let your conversation be always full of grace, seasoned with salt, so that you may know how to answer everyone" (Colossians 4:6). This is the servant mind and spirit that should attend Christian witnessing. The church must see sinners as potential trophies of God's grace, not as objects for evangelistic

151

achievement. They are people whose lives will be enriched through the fellowship of the church.

Yes, there is a balm in Gilead, there is a Physician who has compassion and sees behind the masks worn by the people who are hurting. He besought His embryonic church of chosen disciples to pray for workers who would be sent into His harvest (Matthew 9:37–38). He revealed His Messiahship by "healing every disease and sickness" without discrimination, although His primary purpose was to teach and preach the good news of the kingdom (9:35). His authority was to redeem humankind eternally—body, soul and spirit—as the prophets had foreseen, not merely to meet physical needs, though the physical needs, too, concerned Him.

Keith M. Bailey, in his book, *The Children's Bread,* observes two aspects of divine healing. He writes of what he calls "sign miracles"—"acts to demonstrate God's power and to confirm the gospel." Those acquainted with the history of modern missions know that at times when the gospel has entered new territories under demonic control miraculous mass healings have attended such efforts. The same demonstrative power has diminished dramatically as churches became established. Phenomena like this occur infrequently and are an exception to the principle of Christian healing which Bailey, quoting Jesus (Mark 7:27), calls "children's bread."[1]

It is not the purpose of this book to analyze the complex doctrine of divine healing for disease and sickness. But evangelism is a portrayal of divine healing applicable to the whole person. Evangelism is inadequate without a perceived need for whole-life transformation through sanctification and healing. Conversion is simply the initial step. The church has been given an urgent healing ministry to terminally ill people. But it also has been given the command: "Make disciples!" Its healing ministry is Christ in His saving power being manifest through the church's demonstration of discipleship. "Follow me," said Jesus, "and I will make you fishers of men" (Matthew

4:19). Effective evangelism is both a demonstration and a result of discipleship. Techniques and methods are helpful, but they are not primary.

The effective healing ministry of the church begins when God's servants are aware of, and feel compassion for, people's needs. The spiritual miracle of the new birth may well be accompanied, or followed, by emotional and even physical healing. Christ-like compassion is concerned for a person's whole life, not just his or her eternal destiny, paramount though that is.

The Church as a Healing Fellowship

Regardless of the variety of spiritual gifts in a given church and how many may have the gift of evangelism, if faith, hope and love prevail, members corporately as well as individually will be witnesses to the world of lost people around them. Witness and evangelism are not simply one segment of the church's ministry; they are the church's primary calling as it represents Christ. An uncaring church is not Christlike. The church must perceive itself as a servant of Christ having a healing ministry to hurting people.

The church's ministry of healing must function among its own members who live in fellowship with each other. The roots for divine healing among God's chosen people reach back at least to Abraham and Sarah. God promised Abraham that all the nations of earth would be blessed through his posterity. But there was a problem: Abraham had no posterity. And Sarah, his wife, like Abraham, was by then up in years—Abraham 75, Sarah 65. As if that were not enough, God delayed the promised pregnancy another 24 years! Call it divine healing, call it miracle, but it happened, just as God had promised.

But in Abraham's experience there is an important principle about healing that recurs again and again in the Scriptures: *God's intervention in the physical, material world is incidental to His higher purposes. God does not heal simply to demonstrate that He can.* In this case, God enabled Sarah to have a child so that He could fulfill His purpose to bless the world through Abraham's seed.

Abraham offers us another lesson concerning healing. Long before the birth of Isaac, nomadic Abraham plotted a coexistence with Abimelech, a tribal chieftain, because Abraham's large herds threatened Abimelech's holdings. The arrangement involved Sarah, who would join Abimelech's harem. Abraham introduced Sarah to Abimelech as his sister. Of course, she was in fact his wife and only his half-sister.

God had important plans for Sarah, and being in Abimelech's harem was not among them. So God made the males of Abimelech's household impotent and the women barren. When Abraham's duplicity was discovered and confessed, Abraham prayed for healing and the restoration of Abimelech's household. And Abimelech, who seems to have been a God-fearing man, restored Sarah to Abraham. *Sin* prompted God to send physical dysfunction to Abimelech's desert sheikdom; when Abraham confessed, God brought healing.

God's Covenant at Marah

Consider another example: the bitter water at Marah soon after the Israelites had crossed the Red Sea. Not only did the Lord tell Moses how to "heal" the unpotable water, but He also gave instructions for Israel's continued physical health. The miracle of healing enabled Israel to survive at a time when the entire company sorely needed life-sustaining water. The longer term promise would be crucial to Israel's spiritual walk with God:

> *"If you listen carefully to the voice of the Lord your God and do what is right in his eyes, if you pay attention to his commands and keep all his decrees, I will not bring on you any of the diseases I brought on the Egyptians, for I am the LORD, who heals you."*

(Exodus 15:26)

God was most concerned that Israel walk with Him in obedience. The twin miracles of physical health and physical sustenance would be incidental to that higher divine purpose. Israel's redemption from Egypt was holistic: it was physical, it was spiritual. In God's plan it set the nation apart for His global purposes. God's miracle of preemptive healing—health—was for His higher design to make of Israel a witness to the nations and to bring from Israel His promised Messiah.

Isaiah, Israel's greatest writing prophet, highlights for his people God's promise of healing when he quotes God saying:

> Comfort, comfort my people,
>   says your God.
> Speak tenderly to Jerusalem,
>   and proclaim to her
> that her hard service has been completed,
>   that her sin has been paid for,
> that she has received from the LORD's hand
>   double for all her sins.
>   (Isaiah 40:1–2)

Franz Delitzsch, in his commentary on Isaiah, observes that the phrase, "double for all her sins," should not be understood judicially. "Jerusalem had not suffered more than its sins had deserved," Delitzsch says, "but the compassion of God regarded what His justice had been obligated to inflict upon Jerusalem as superabundant."[2]

Healing in the New Covenant

God's healing ordinance for Israel, delivered at Marah, forms a background on which divine healing for His New Covenant people is biblically portrayed. Physical affliction may be God's judgment for some sin, as, for example, the "weak and sick" Corinthians who had abused the Lord's Table (1 Corinthians 11:30). In such instances, confession and changed behavior are the first steps to healing. But there are non-judgmental afflictions as well. Provision for these is part of God's shepherding care and superabundant grace. After Isaiah makes his prophetic announcement of John the Baptist's ministry, he has these words:

> *See, the Sovereign LORD comes with power,*
> *and his arm rules for him.*
> *See, his reward is with him,*
> *and his recompense accompanies him.*
> *He tends his flock like a shepherd:*
> *He gathers the lambs in his arms*
> *and carries them close to his heart;*
> *he gently leads those that have young.*
> (Isaiah 40:10–11)

Spiritually and emotionally, as well as physically, God's redeemed Old Testament saints—and the church in prophetic foregleam—are represented as a flock under the superabundant compassion of a sovereign Shepherd. God ministers to them His own health care; as His flock, they prosper.

As we saw in chapter 7, the New Testament offers a number of "each-other/one-another" exhortations defining the caring relation church members should have for each other. One of these is in James: "Therefore confess your sins to each other and pray for each other so that you may be healed. The prayer of a righteous man is powerful and effective" (James 5:16). Relational health and healing is to grace the church because of God's abounding mercy. What church members experience vertically in a sanctified relationship to God they reflect horizontally in the sanctified relationship of a peoplehood.

The simple instruction James offers for physical healing runs parallel with his instruction for those who may be in trouble (5:13). Emotions such as happiness or stress are important factors in believers' well-being. The church is to keep the whole person in its purview. It is to be a house of healing for believers, a place where they can experience God's comfort and blessing. Paul writes to the Colossians:

> As God's chosen people, holy and dearly loved, clothe yourselves with compassion, kindness, humility, gentleness and patience. Bear with each other and forgive whatever grievances you may have against one another. Forgive as the Lord forgave you. And over all these virtues put on love, which binds them all together in perfect unity.
>
> Let the peace of Christ rule in your hearts, since as members of one body you were called to peace. And be thankful. Let the word of Christ dwell in you richly as you teach and admonish one another with all wisdom, and as you sing psalms, hymns and spiritual songs with gratitude in your hearts to God.
>
> (Colossians 3:12–16)

A Dwelling Place of God

Throughout Scripture but particularly in the New Testament, God has wanted to have a healing, loving, peaceful relationship with His people. And He has wanted to see similar accord as His people relate to each other. In this church age He has gone a giant step farther: He indwells the church by His Spirit to facilitate His objectives. That is why Paul, referring to the church, uses such terms as "temple," "house," "habitation," "abode"—God lives among us! And when we experience the fullness of His shepherding relationship, we relate to our fellow members in expressions of Christ's abounding grace, including physical healing. Christ's death at Calvary in atonement for our sins is the basis for His abundant grace among us, His people. It is "the children's bread."   The healing that comes with sanctifying grace ministered within Christian fellowship is more than a natural catharsis. It is the sharing of divine life that flows because of Christ's finished atonement: "If the Spirit of him who raised Jesus from the dead is living in you, he who raised Christ from the dead will also give life to your mortal bodies through his Spirit, who lives in you" (Romans 8:11). It is a promise that carries eschatological dimensions, but it is also for the present and has both spiritual and physical dimensions.

We too much tend to consider physical healing an individual thing with neither a church setting nor a higher spiritual purpose. Healing is simply something that happenstance demands. But the Scriptures put healing within a corporate context in which healing, if granted, serves a higher spiritual purpose. When Paul wrote about "the Spirit of him who raised Christ from the dead [giving] life to your mortal bodies" (Romans 8:11), he was addressing a corporate church in Rome. For that corporate church God had a ministry of high purpose: God intended them "to be conformed to the likeness of his Son" (8:29).

Undoubtedly the reference to Gaius, mentioned in Third John, has behind it a similar corporate purpose. John prayed for his "dear friend Gaius," a beloved church leader, "that you may enjoy good health and that all may go well with you, even as your soul is getting along well" (3 John 2). John had been told how Gaius was "walking in the truth,"—apparently setting the pace in Christian leadership by his exposition and application of God's Word in the church. It was a reflection of his own walk in the truth. Now itinerant evangelists who had been visiting the church would soon depart, and John, who had a special concern for the churches in Asia Minor, encouraged Gaius to "send them on their way in a manner worthy of God" (verse 6).

There is a generosity "worthy of God" that fosters physical, emotional and spiritual health. This is not the cheap "health and wealth" gospel being promoted by some of the televangelists and pulpiteers. Psychologists and other doctors recognize that physical illness frequently has an emotional component. What these doctors usually overlook is the *spiritual* component also present. When the whole church body ministers to the whole person's need in a manner "worthy of God" and His kingdom purpose, healing and health will grace that loving fellowship.

Healing amid Spiritual Conflict and Challenge

As Jesus' incarnate ministry needs to be seen from the higher perspective of His death and resurrection, so also must the church's ministry and sufferings be seen. The big picture of God's purpose is often incomprehensible to us.

James stresses perseverance in suffering. The righteous are not exempt from suffering in a fallen world. Believers, like unbelievers, groan and travail for the day of redemption. But mere escape from suffering is unworthy of God's honor. James refers to Job and his perseverance. There is no indication that the patriarch knew what had transpired in the heavenlies to provoke his chain of calamities and his intense suffering. As far as we know, God may not ever have divulged to Job in Job's long lifetime the heavenly conversation between God and Satan.

Before disaster struck, Job had been especially shielded from harm. Under God's sovereign goodness, the work of Job's hands had been singularly blessed. He was on display before God, before angels—and before Satan and his demons—as a man of faith and impeccable character. To his—and God's—eternal credit, Job emerged from the conflict refined, but still faithful, still a man of impeccable character. The conflict endured by Job at least four millennia ago still continues in the universe.

For Paul, the gift of God's grace in his ministry to the Gentiles utterly amazed him. He explains it in these words: "[God's] intent was that now, through the church, the manifold wisdom of God should be made known to the rulers and authorities in the heavenly realms, according to his eternal purpose which he accomplished in Christ Jesus our Lord" (Ephesians 3:10–11). Yet despite the riches of God's grace, the apostle was challenged by severe conflict and physical suffering. But he did not lose heart. His focus was on Jesus Christ Himself coming in glory and power for His bride, the church, radiant and complete (Ephesians 5:15–32). The big picture of the church had captured Paul's vision. Most of his letters provide developing insight regarding the way the church, equipped to advance the kingdom universally, should function. They also warn of heightened conflict and challenging times of persecution and suffering.

Varied Methods, Consistent Purpose

When Jesus healed physical ailments, He varied His methods, but He consistently served a kingdom purpose. In our day of technology and scientific method, we are constantly looking for consistent patterns and predictability. We want to "harness the laws of nature." In the church, when it comes to divine healing, we tend to adopt a similar methodology. We want to "harness" divine healing. Craze for methodology usually leads to unbiblical dogmatism and fanaticism that are not Christlike. The big picture does not permit us to take such an approach. It puts Christ and His universal purpose out of focus.

The miracles of Jesus were spontaneous. They were suitable for a particular occasion of need. Jesus did not mean for His methods to set a precedent. Nor is there any record of Peter's shadow (Acts 5:15) or the handkerchiefs and aprons that touched Paul (Acts 19:12) being repeated.

Although Jesus Christ is the same yesterday, today and forever (Hebrews 13:8), His ways are inscrutable. At the same time His resurrection power is known by those who seek to be made conformable to His death. Those who miss the spirit of Jesus' ministry and seek to imitate merely His healing methods are likely to be hucksters who bargain for reputation and material gain. Paul identified himself with his colaborers when he wrote: "We always carry around in our body the death of Jesus, so that the life of Jesus may also be revealed in our body" (2 Corinthians 4:10).

It is instructive that Paul did not set out to hold healing campaigns to advance the gospel. Healing at times occurred as Paul preached the gospel. But physical healing is never a forefront feature in the Acts or in the Letters. It is not a primary element in the larger picture of apostolic ministry. The larger picture introduces challenge in which God's kingdom purpose is being fulfilled.

In almost 20 centuries of church history no particular church or denomination has become a model of immunity from the calamities, sicknesses and diseases which man's fall has generated. On the other hand, hardly any extended period of church history has been without some demonstration of divine healing for physical bodies.[3]

Manifestations of divine physical healings have occurred particularly in periods when new directions of God's kingdom-working developed, whether in biblical history or in church history. The lack of uniformity in this phenomenon seems to emphasize the unique nature of these outbreaks.[4]

No particular church or denomination has a corner on what Bailey prefers to call Christian healing. Miracle manifestations of physical healings seem to belong to the larger picture and higher purpose of world evangelization, even though physical healings do take place in assemblies that exercise faith for physical healing.

The human search for models or patterns in an effort to make a show of miracle power in physical healing often excludes the primary significance of the spiritual. If God allowed a messenger of Satan to be a thorn in Paul's flesh in order to prove the sufficiency of His grace, should we not expect the same possibility? Furthermore, Christ's constant intercession for us and the miracles of His care and protection far outnumber—and likely are far more crucial—than the manifestations of healing that we observe.

Choice Servants, Special Targets

Satan makes God's choice servants his special targets. He "accuses them before our God day and night" (Revelation 12:10), even as Old Testament Job was targeted and accused. We do not fully realize the wisdom of the prayer Jesus taught His disciples to pray:

> *Our Father in heaven,*
> *hallowed be your name,*
> *your kingdom come,*
> *your will be done*
>   *on earth as it is in heaven.*
> *Give us today our daily bread.*
> *Forgive us our debts,*
>   *as we also have forgiven our debtors.*
> *And lead us not into temptation,*
>   *but deliver us from the evil one.*
> (Matthew 6:9–13)

The person who walks daily in the faith of this prayer is aware of God's compassion, presence and power to deliver him or her from the evil one. The person whose Christian walk is at best casual and whose faith is shallow may be oblivious to the surrounding danger and the stress of satanic affliction he or she experiences. In either case, the corporate church, if it is functioning biblically, will discern God's mind concerning the distressed member and exercise appropriate care.

For God's healing to take place, the church needs the message of God's healing and, as James says, a spirit of forgiveness. Surely it also needs demonstrations of physical healing as "children's bread," but never to the exclusion of primarily meeting spiritual needs and discerning when suffering is purposeful. The psalmist reminds Israel (and us) that in the desert God gave His people what they craved for but "sent a wasting disease upon them" (Psalm 106:15).

Divine healing is not a panacea. It must not be an escape from spiritual discipline designed by God to perfect the believer's relationship with Him. Sometimes we suffer to enable us to identify with others who suffer (2 Corinthians 1:6). Sometimes we suffer "according to God's will" (1 Peter 4:19). Christ Himself "learned obedience from what he suffered" (Hebrews 5:8).

Paul triumphed in spirit despite physical conflict and suffering. He says:

> We have this treasure in jars of clay to show that this all-surpassing power is from God and not from us. We are hard pressed on every side, but not crushed; perplexed, but not in despair; persecuted, but not abandoned; struck down, but not destroyed. We always carry around in our body the death of Jesus, so that the life of Jesus may also be revealed in our body.
>
> (2 Corinthians 4:7–10)

Seeing the Big Picture

Scoffers are prone to ask, "Where was Christ while Paul was suffering?" But physical healing and overt divine intervention are not necessarily appropriate to the larger picture. The physical sufferings Paul endured were incidental to the daily pressure of his concern for all the churches. He explains: "For we who are alive are always being given over to death for Jesus' sake, so that his life may be revealed in our mortal body. So then, death is at work in us, but life is at work in you" (2 Corinthians 4:11–12).

The challenge of Paul's life was that churches might be established and matured, that Christ might be glorified and His power manifest in his dedication, whether by a life of suffering or by death. There was a mighty Intelligence behind Paul's reckless abandon to Christ. Both his personal suffering and his healing ministry to others fitted a larger, more important picture.

While God's choice servant suffered, miracles of healing called sinners to repentance. Paul was shipwrecked, floating on planks in a raging storm to save his life. Later he was bitten by a viper while seeking relief from the wet and cold. Yet afterward the pagan islanders of Malta were healed: "The rest of the sick on the island came and were cured" (Acts 28:9). Paul was not overcome with self-pity by the contrast of his sufferings and the well-being of these who found miraculous health. Instead, he glorified God.

Because Paul knew and trusted Christ, he did not need to comprehend all the "whys and wherefores." He saw himself and the other apostles "on display at the end of the procession, like men condemned to die in the arena" (1 Corinthians 4:9). In his dedicated obedience he could only say to the Corinthians, "I urge you to imitate me" (4:16).

At the same time, Paul could discern physical sickness and even death because of spiritually unhealthy conditions in the Corinth church (1 Corinthians 11:28–31). God's grace was at work individually and corporately to spare believers from being "condemned with the world" (1 Corinthians 11:32).

Intelligent and informed faith sees the larger picture. Believers must know the ground of their faith. They must contend for a healthy faith in the body-life of the church. Without the spirit of servanthood spoken of in chapter 7, it is doubtful that much healing will take place in the church, or that the corporate believers will be a healthy body.

In a fallen world, the righteous are not exempt from suffering. Believers groan and travail for the day of redemption. What makes the church work with effectiveness is prayer. God's will is to be performed on earth as it is in heaven. His healing power is present as believers stand in the righteousness of Christ and claim His compassion and grace for each other. Healing is a vital part of the church's ministry to the terminally ill in soul, to the needy within the church fellowship and for those who suffer in their conflict with Satan.

Christ intended for His church to have a healing ministry to the whole person: spirit, soul and body. This will be reflected in its worship, in its sense of commission, in its nurture and in its success in conserving converts. Discipleship will largely be the result of proper training and the kind of teaching that comes from demonstrated consecration and dedication. Its evangelism and commitment will also result in missions and the cultivation of contacts as the "going" becomes a consistent walk with God. The sanctification of believers personally will be reflected in the sanctifying ministry of the church corporately.

To know Christ as Savior, Sanctifier, Healer and coming King is to believe in His abounding fullness for redemption, including His power to heal to the full extent of humankind's fall. It is fitting that Christ should be known as Savior and Sanctifier so that He may be known also among God's people as Healer. But perfect wholeness will only be known as the church is caught up to meet, and fully transformed by, its coming King.

Endnotes

[1] Keith M. Bailey, *The Children's Bread* (Harrisburg: Christian Publications, 1977), p. 29.

[2] Franz Delitzsch, *The Prophecies of Isaiah*, Vol. 2 (Grand Rapids: Wm. B. Eerdmans Publishing Co., 1954), p. 140.

[3] A.J. Gordon in his book, *The Ministry of Healing* (Harrisburg: Christian Publications, n.d.), traces the ministry of healing since the New Testament canon (chapter 3). Keith Bailey, in *The Children's Bread* (see note 1 above), provides a similar resume (chapter 12), and in a following chapter he analyzes the modern healing movements. These writers establish historical testimony that the church has experienced miracle healings for the body in modern church history.

[4]Both throughout biblical history and in church history miracles of physical healing appear to introduce transitions in God's working. The patriarchal period, Israel's national beginning after deliverance from Egypt, the period of the kings and prophets, the incarnational ministry of Jesus, the birth of the church at Pentecost, the Reformation and the modern evangelical movement all seem to demonstrate this. The Christian and Missionary Alliance with its emphasis on divine healing has its historical roots in the middle of the 19th century and the ministries of Johannes Blumhardt, Dorthea Trudel, Otto Stockmayer, W.E. Boardman, Charles Spurgeon, Charles Cullis, Andrew Murray and A.J. Gordon as well as Albert Simpson. The showmanship and miracle-mongering often portrayed on television today are quite different from what took place in these other periods.

9

The Leaders
of the Church

God has chosen His servant peoplehood—the church—to reach the world with the gospel. God has neither canceled the church's role nor relieved it of obligation. The pressures of an unbelieving world have only strengthened its resolve. Creeds, emerging out of severe testing, have defined its orthodoxy. The church's foundation is firm, and it moves forward.

This is not to suggest that the church is without dysfunction. Even rudimentary familiarity with the New Testament and church history quickly dispel any such illusion. Peter acknowledged the church's imperfection.

He writes: "It is time for judgment to begin with the family of God; and if it begins with us, what will the outcome be for those who do not obey the gospel of God?" (1 Peter 4:17). The church is a divine family-center where truth is anchored in discipline. From that center the church reaches out into its community, into its world. From that center God raises up leaders whom He calls into ministry.

As the church lives the truth and is led by the truth, it will attract corresponding obedience to the gospel from those outside the church. The church is not simply a medium of communication. It is, by its very existence and body life, a message. Will the watching world embrace Truth—Truth with a capital "T"—or will it face judgment? Often far beyond our immediate awareness, the Holy Spirit is "convict[ing] the world of guilt in regard to sin and righteousness and judgment" (John 16:8).

Jesus came without reputation into a sin-ridden world, to His own people smothered by 400 silent years of vain religious tradition. He came to bring justice and judgment (John 9:39). He relinquished all His rights and privileges in order to identify with the seemingly forgotten remnant of a once prosperous nation.

Through obedience Jesus affirmed God's universal judgment, died on the cross to effect redemption, arose to empower His church and deputized His disciples with a universal gospel. God's universal judgment will continue to prevail from His universal church (and the local churches that represent it) until His redemptive plan is complete. "There is one body and one Spirit—just as you were called to one hope when you were called—one Lord, one faith, one baptism; one God and Father of all, who is over all and through all and in all" (Ephesians 4:4–6).[1]

The church as "God's household," "the pillar and foundation of the truth" (1 Timothy 3:15), is the primary locus for the outworking of doctrine, discipline and ministry. It is God's primary agency for redemption. But the church cannot fulfill these roles without divinely ordained and appointed leaders. In the context and vortex of a chosen peoplehood, leaders are needed to teach, to preach and to "prepare God's people for works of service" (Ephesians 4:12).

Leadership Is a Call to Servanthood

The Old Testament prophets—we could call them leaders—ministered to Israel to form a faithful remnant who would serve God's plan of redemption. In the New Covenant brought in by Jesus Christ, this faithful remnant of the Old Covenant joined the followers of Jesus in a new peoplehood, the church. The church, comprised first of Jews and, later, Gentiles as well, began its global stewardship. The apostles, prepared as leaders by Jesus, became foundation lay-ers of this church, a church entrusted with a divine glory, the services of worship, the promises of redemption and the divine covenants first given to Israel.

The apostolic leaders were not isolated individualists. They had been especially called by God to spearhead the church's first assault on a world firmly in Satan's grip. But there were others as well. Paul interprets to the predominantly Gentile church in Ephesus the Messianic meaning of a verse in Psalm 68. He writes: "When he ascended on high, / he led captives in his train / and gave gifts to men" (Ephesians 4:8). The "he" is Christ. And the gifts? They were gifts of leadership for the church:

> He . . . gave some to be apostles, some to be prophets, some to be evangelists, and some to be pastors and teachers, to prepare God's people for works of service, so that the body of Christ may be built up until we all reach unity in the faith and in the knowledge of the Son of God and become mature, attaining to the whole measure of the fullness of Christ.
> (Ephesians 4:11–13)

God positions divinely commissioned leaders to equip His people (the church) for works of service. Christ through His intercessory ministry provides service gifts for the church which the Holy Spirit apportions to each member as He determines (1 Corinthians 12:11). Discipleship without works of service is an anomaly, like a bird that cannot fly.

Through mutual faith in God's mercy and power, these gifted first century leaders and the prepared and gifted people they led were to evangelize the world for Christ. And that pattern applies yet. God has indicated no change in the plan He has so clearly spelled out for us in the New Testament.

Apostles are akin to missionaries (both words connote someone sent on assignment). In addition to Paul and the other apostles, a number of New Testament leaders exercised that function: Barnabas (Acts 13:2), Mark and Silas (Acts 15:39–40), Titus (2 Corinthians 8:23), Timothy (1 Timothy 1:3)—to name some. Usually missionaries are sent to people bereft of the gospel. Their ministry is made possible through the financial and prayer support of a church base. Prayer, money and mutual faith undergird their ministry.

New Covenant *prophets* are called to minister the sanctifying grace of Christ to the churches, to strengthen the church and solidify its core of commitment.

Evangelists are called to inspire and model a passion for the lost in the community where the church ministers.

Pastors and *teachers* are called to shepherd a local church, to teach the Word of God, to give spiritual direction, to inspire and lead the church in its acts of service.

No Place for Elitism

The church commissions its leaders, and the leaders submit to the church even as all members submit to one another and in service to the Lord. The New Testament church is God's base for ministry, and its major effectiveness is in the whole body. The church has been given gifts, and these are important, but the main attention is not on the gifts but on the body as a whole and the maturity that fits it for acts of service.

The New Testament picture of the church is of an ever-multiplying, ever-spreading organism. Its rank-and-file members are at various levels of maturity. Dedicated leaders, working within the church structure, in depend-ence upon God are endeavoring to bring them to maturity. Among the apostles, and even in the lesser levels of leadership, there is little hint of elitism, Diotrephes (3 John 9) being possibly the only exception. Even Paul, despite his prominence and authority, comes across as the servant of Jesus Christ that he claims again and again to be.

The danger of elitism and heroism is loss of corporate servanthood. By nature, leaders tend to redesign the church around their self-image. They forget they are only one part of the whole body and they belong to all the others (Romans 12:5). They lose sight of the fact that they, too, however seasoned, have some maturing to do "until we all reach unity in the faith, . . . attaining to the whole measure of the fullness of Christ" (Ephesians 4:13).

John the Baptist's martyrdom predated the church by perhaps three years, but he sets a beautiful example for the church. When some of John's disciples observed that Jesus was upstaging him, John was unperturbed. "A man can receive only what is given him from heaven," John answered. "He must become greater; I must become less" (John 3:27, 30).

When leaders assume self-importance, lording it over the church, there is a shift in focus and a shift in attitude. The focus of the church members shifts from the core-center where Christ is Head. And the members no longer regard themselves as a gifted body existing for the com-mon good.

Servants in the body need leaders, but leaders ultimately succeed only through self-giving, not self-serving. "Christ loved the church and gave himself up for her to make her holy, cleansing her by the washing with water through the word" (Ephesians 5:25–26).

Of his own leadership in the church, Paul has this to say:

> Now I rejoice in what was suffered for you, and I fill up in my flesh what is still lacking in regard to Christ's afflictions, for the sake of his body, which is the church. I have become its servant by the commission God gave me to present to you the word of God in its fullness—the mystery that has been kept hidden for ages and generations, but is now disclosed to the saints. To them God has chosen to make known among the Gentiles the glorious riches of this mystery, which is Christ in you, the hope of glory.
> (Colossians 1:24–27)

Paul's agenda for ministry began with the church, despite his capacity for effective ministry and potential heroism. Paul recognized the fullness of Christ indwelling the church and maturing its members as the most effective means to extend the gospel to Gentiles outside of Christ. He so identified himself with the church and its life-center as to envision the church "building itself up" qualitatively and then quantitatively (Ephesians 4:12–13). Paul would willingly suffer for what was lacking in regard to Christ's afflictions for the church so that every member might live in union with Christ for a lost world.

Leadership is a call to servanthood with the body, not to heroism or to popularity.

Leadership Is a Call to Unity

Where there are no followers, there can be no leaders. Unless the ministry of leaders produces purposeful unity and motivation, it eventually fails. But spiritual leadership finds its strength in union with Christ and in identification with His plan of redemption through the church. Genuine unity and authentic leadership in such a context have a divine dimension that cannot be duplicated by secular societies.

In His high priestly prayer Jesus prays that those who would believe in Him through the message of His disciples might be one "so that the world may believe that you have sent me. . . ." Jesus continues: "May they be brought to complete unity to let the world know that you sent me and have loved them even as you have loved me" (John 17:21, 23). For His church Jesus envisioned both a concentric expansion and a cyclical succession. This would come through the dynamic relationship of member unity and message proclamation, convincing an unregenerate world that God had sent His Son and that they should trust His love for them.

Note the continuity of leadership: Father to Son, Son to apostles, apostles to church. Christ Himself, however, gives gifts of leadership to the church. As the church develops maturity, the model and message of the God-given leaders equip the rank-and-file members for corporate service. The church should be the training ground where future leaders develop their gifts. Christ, through the Holy Spirit, coordinates and integrates the gifts and services of the members.

Leadership is crucial to the church. It should exemplify a call to unity. Its greatest challenge is to bring solidarity and oneness with Christ to the church. This unity is divine. Its source is through knowing Christ and obeying God's Word. It cannot be fabricated by human ingenuity and manipulation.

Throughout the New Testament we find the unity of the church threatened: John and Peter, two key leaders, are jailed and forbidden to speak about Jesus (Acts 4:3, 18). Ananias and Sapphira plot to deceive the church (5:1–2). Grecian widows are neglected in the distribution of food (6:1). The Apostles are too overloaded to give their attention "to prayer and the ministry of the word" (6:4). The list goes on and on.

Almost from the beginning, the church was threatened by hard-line "Judaizers" who insisted that Gentile Christians must keep the Mosaic law. Self-serving heretics within the Corinthian church denied the resurrection of the dead. Some in the church at Thessalonica, presuming the Lord would return momentarily, had quit their jobs and were a financial burden to fellow believers. The Philippian church was distracted by a disagreement between two of its women, Syntyche and Euodia. Docetism—the view that Jesus Christ was not actually human—had infected the Colossian assembly.

In every case, leadership was crucial lest these doctrinal and spiritual problems totally damage the unity so essential to a properly functioning church. Without leadership, unity is not possible. Without unity, the church becomes dysfunctional, spiritually paralyzed and vulnerable to the enemy.

The Heart as Well as the Head

We have a tendency to suppose that all we need for unity is a code of correct doctrine. If we are biblical, the argument runs, we are united. Although the Scriptures expect doctrinal consistency, the threats to unity within the New Testament church more often hinged on obedience than on beliefs. It was not complex philosophical argument that the church or its troublesome members needed but rather a spiritual recall to obedience—obedience to Christ.

Our modern culture is riddled by deviate rationalization. All too frequently it is simply a camouflage for disobedient hearts. In their trouble-shooting, church leaders need to know where to look. Truth is not relative. It is absolute; it is exclusive. It can be expressed in sound doctrine. It will also be expressed through human personality and character.

To the complicated Pharisees, Jesus appeared doctrinally inconsistent. But He was consistent with the Word and in step with His Father's will and purpose. Leaders who, like the Pharisees, pour themselves into complex and rigid creeds find their minds becoming warped, their motives skewed. Paul warns Timothy against those who have "an unhealthy interest in controversies and quarrels about words that result in envy, strife, malicious talk, evil suspicions and constant friction between men of corrupt mind" (1 Timothy 6:4–5).

Simpson had to let God remove from him some of the accretion of rigid religious tradition in order for the freshness of the gospel to come alive to him. Christ in His fullness became a transforming reality, a unifying force. From that dynamic was launched The Christian and Missionary Alliance. Simpson befuddled Arminians and Calvinists, refusing to be drawn into their debate. It was sinful, in Simpson's view, to be part of a religious faction bred out of an unhealthy interest in controversies and arguments.

Paul's warnings rightly assume that disunity originates with factious leaders and people's cunning—a schema of human ingenuity that departs from the simplicity found in Christ Jesus. Paul's warnings often are followed by exhortations to cohesive obedience. For example, Paul says to the Ephesians: "Instead, speaking the truth in love, . . . in all things grow up into him who is the Head, that is, Christ. From him the whole body, joined and held together by every supporting ligament, grows and builds itself up in love, as each part does its work" (Ephesians 4:15–16).

Unity substantiates the gospel. Truth and function have an inner connection that must not be distracted from either the church's giving center or from Christ its Head. Conflict can be constructive—if it is on the outside. Even internal conflict can result in stronger unity and more worthy motives. But when the integrity of the church and its very purposes are at stake, discipline becomes essential.[2]

Functional and Spiritual Unity

The church needs doctrinal unity. God expects believers to take a stand on what they believe. At the same time, they must be willing to examine all perspectives critically with the mind of Christ and in the light of His Word lest they quench the Spirit's flame. Paul tells the Thessalonians: "Do not put out the Spirit's fire; do not treat prophecies with contempt. Test everything. Hold on to the good" (1 Thessalonians 5:19–21).

The church also needs functional unity and, most of all, spiritual unity—a unity that will combine Word and deed in faithful servanthood. To produce spiritual unity, church leaders must develop the mind of Christ within the church body. This was Paul's emphatic purpose in his letter to the Corinthians. He says to them (and he is speaking to the corporate church): "Don't you know that you yourselves are God's temple and that God's Spirit lives in you? If anyone destroys God's temple, God will destroy him; for God's temple is sacred, and you are that temple" (1 Corinthians 3:16–17).

Church unity thrives under godly, faithful leaders. Church unity is most vulnerable under the wrong leaders. Paul urged the Roman church "to watch out for those who cause divisions and put obstacles in your way that are contrary to the teaching you have learned. Keep away from them. For such people are not serving our Lord Christ, but their own appetites" (Romans 16:17–18).

The church that fails to develop leaders from its concentric base and declines its responsibility to hone the leaders it has is refusing its highest challenge for the future. The statement is true for local churches and true for denominations of local churches.

The qualities important in North American church leaders apply to missionary leaders. Missionaries are important representatives of the church or churches from which they have been sent. The Lord has constituted "home" churches to be mediating authorities to their missionary representatives. Missionaries hold in mutual trust with their home church that church's doctrines, its worshipful spirit of service, its responsibility to obey the Great Commission. Proper coordination and interdependence between a church and its missionaries greatly strengthens both church and missionaries. There is unity of purpose and spirit. The church sees missions as a primary part of its total function.

The Christian and Missionary Alliance accepts constituted authority as a principle of unity. "Obey your leaders and submit to their authority," says the writer of Hebrews to the church he is writing to. "They keep watch over you as men who must give an account. Obey them so that their work will be a joy, not a burden, for that would be of no advantage to you" (Hebrews 13:17). The Bible fosters a decorum of respect and honor that allows issues to be aired in proper forum uninhibiting to personal integrity. Constituted authority can incorporate flexibility and openness within a spirit of Christian fellowship that encourages a mutually established trust.

Unity is more than a noble ideal. It often requires courage and honest confrontation in a spirit of love. Unity is not bland or undefined, nor does it compromise for the sake of compromising. It fosters mutual trust in Christ and His Word to produce form and character along with constituted authority. A spiritual leader has an allegiance to the church, the body of Christ; his or her calling is to foster unity and maturity within the body and to encourage the church to "works of service."

Leadership Is a Call to Vision

Leadership and vision have mutual overtones. Leaders are called to lead, but a leader's vision largely determines in what direction. Consider Moses at the burning bush (Exodus 3). What caught Moses' attention was not the fire—he had seen bushes burn before—but that the bush was not consumed (3:2–3). If "this strange sight" is of God, it is usually a demanding call, unachievable by natural means, a test of faith and courage that positions a leader on holy ground (3:5). Moses is described by the writer of Hebrews as one who "persevered because he saw him who is invisible" (Hebrews 11:27). Old Testament prophets were called "seers"—men of God who saw more and farther than ordinary men, an enlightenment and a conviction of divine origin.

As with Moses, responding to God's leading and timing with careful steps of obedience is necessary to fulfill a vision. The "vision" must be validated in providence (sometimes personal desires are mistaken for visions) and in the hearts of those who will participate in it. If they are to be worthy partners in the vision, they, too, must own it.

Forty years later God laid on Joshua the mantle Moses had taken up so reluctantly but borne so well. God told Joshua:

> *"Be strong and courageous, because you will lead these people to inherit the land I swore to their forefathers to give them. Be strong and very courageous. Be careful to obey all the law my servant Moses gave you; do not turn from it to the right or to the left, that you may be successful wherever you go."*
>
> (Joshua 1:6–7)

For many years Joshua had served Moses. Now he stood in Moses' position. Rather than to compare himself with Moses, he had to keep his eyes on God and trust God's Word. Inheriting the land would require vision with endurance and great courage.

Visionless leadership is self-contradictory. By definition true leaders are people of vision. Jesus saw the multitudes, like sheep without a shepherd, and envisioned their gathering into His fold (John 10:11–13). He foresaw Peter as Pentecostal spokesman and gave him the keys of the kingdom (Matthew 16:19).

Hear Paul's vision for the church at Ephesus as he gathers its elders at Miletus on his trip from Corinth to Jerusalem:

> "Keep watch over yourselves and all the flock of which the Holy Spirit has made you overseers. Be shepherds of the church of God, which he bought with his own blood. . . .
> I commit you to God and to the word of his grace, which can build you up and give you an inheritance among all those who are sanctified."
> (Acts 20:28, 32)

Divinely appointed leaders must provide visionary oversight to lead their flock into the inheritance God has ordained for them. Visions are not flash-in-the-pan ventures inspired by wishful thinking or mere derring-do. They are the result of faithful obedience to the implanted Word and an intimate acquaintance with God. Leadership under trial only succeeds through prayer and patient faith. It is a call to endurance.

Leadership Is a Response to Divine Imperatives

Servanthood, unity and vision are important elements of leadership in the church, but none is more important than faith. Leaders must be able to perceive God's purpose and will. This ability comes from an inner ear trained to hear God's voice. There are two tracks on which a spiritual and effective church runs: the Word of God and the Spirit of God. These tracks are always parallel. Unless a church's leaders are aware of, and responsive to, a divine imperative in their personal lives, the church is in danger.

God's call upon people for leadership ministry is personal. But it is also corporate. Paul makes this clear when he speaks of our need "to test and approve what God's will is—his good, pleasing and perfect will" (Romans 12:2). When he goes on to talk about assessing our capabilities "with sober judgment, in accordance with the measure of faith" God has given us (12:3), he has spiritual gifts within the church in mind (see 12:4). If the gift is leadership (12:8), the leader is to "govern diligently." The response of faith, with spiritual vision and obedience to God's Word and Spirit, is foundational to any divine call. Church leaders stepping into office without such are falsely motivated and directed.

In a sense, all members of the body of Christ have gifts that provide some level of leadership as they are exercised under a divine imperative. But there is danger in serving mere programs rather than the Lord Himself, or of having righteous intentions fueled by selfish desires. Without a divine imperative derived from God's Word and the Spirit of God, the whole church is in danger of drifting into the grip of enemy forces. It risks being led by the whim of people who may claim that the Lord spoke to them, but who do not evidence it in spiritual discernment or Spirit-borne guidance.

The true concept of a vision, the gestation of plans and their eventual fulfillment need to be pursued in a spirit of worshipful service. In the process this vision is bathed in prayer and open to the correction and timing of the Holy Spirit. It is He who inspires faith on the part of members to accept the vision. It is He who releases resources for its fulfillment. Little wonder that divinely appointed church leadership is so necessary!

The Scriptures declare that Christ "ascended higher than all the heavens, in order to fill the whole universe" (Ephesians 4:10). Likely God has long-range goals for the church—the bride of Christ— that we little dream of. But for now, the church's mission is two-fold: (1) edification, building its own members toward maturity of faith, and (2) evangelization, taking the Good News of Jesus Christ to those who have not yet responded to it, whether locally or at the ends of the earth.

The Types of Church Leaders

To accomplish this two-part mission, what types of church leaders are called for?

Apostles, *(some may prefer to call them missionaries),* *prophets and evangelists* serve the church at large, or serve churches bonded in mutual fellowship.

Pastors and teachers (so the Greek in Ephesians 4:11, but some prefer to hyphenate the words and call them pastor-teachers) minister chiefly within a local church. Like apostles (missionaries), prophets and evangelists, pastor-teachers are divinely given gifts to the church (again, Ephesians 4:11).[3]

Elders likewise serve within a local fellowship. In New Testament times a plurality of elders seemed to be the custom (see Acts 14:23; Titus 1:5).

The Bible does not put any of the above ministries in rigid categories. Always they are to reflect the primacy of the Word. The fact that the terms are used somewhat interchangeably suggests varying needs within specific churches. For example, Paul implies two classes of elders in one of his letters to Timothy:

> *The elders who direct the affairs of the church well are* *worthy of double honor, especially those whose work is* *preaching and teaching. For the Scripture says, "Do not* *muzzle the ox while it is treading out the grain," and "The* *worker deserves his wages."*
> (1 Timothy 5:17–18)

Here the significance of the Word and the demanding task of preaching and teaching require special recognition. They need to be adequately supported in order to fulfill their divinely appointed function in the church. Peter expresses concern for church elders when he writes:

> *To the elders among you, I appeal as a fellow elder, a* *witness of Christ's sufferings and one who also will share* *in the glory to be revealed: Be shepherds of God's flock that* *is under your care, serving as overseers—not because you* *must, but because you are willing, as God wants you to be;* *not greedy for money, but eager to serve; not lording it over*

those entrusted to you, but being examples to the flock.
(1 Peter 5:1–3)

In this passage Peter's concern is for overseeing elders. He identifies himself as one of them even though he is the leading member among Christ's chosen apostles. *Elders* includes "shepherds of God's flock," or pastor-elders. It includes overseeing elders, a category that may include Peter himself. Overseeing elders may include as well bishops (overseers) who administer a fellowship of churches. Tradition holds that John was bishop over the seven churches in Asia Minor.

Elders (the term refers more to experience than to age) were recognized and chosen leaders of a church. They were mediators of God's rule both in function and spiritual stature. In the New Testament they are the administrators and executors of the church. They are accountable for the purity and stability of the church.

Toward the end of the first century, when the apostles, teachers and prophets no longer were able physically to travel to outlying churches, their functions fell on local elders, among whom an official leader, called a president in post-New Testament writings, was chosen to give his full time to this ministry.

As the passage from First Peter above suggests, in New Testament time status or rank among elders was not an issue. A divine imperative drove the church, and by their manifest accountability to the Lord and to the church, these elders administered the truth of God's Word while overseeing the various ministries of the church.[4]

Deacons and Deaconesses

This background of eldership illuminates our understanding of the offices of deacons and deaconesses. The word *deacon* means "servant," an honorable term applied to Jesus Christ and preferred by Paul the apostle. Like the "overseers" (1 Timothy 3:1–7), deacons must meet high qualifications. Their role is to relieve elders of responsibilities that would distract them from their primary duties. In general terms, this was the role of the first deacons (Acts 6:1–6). Their work, far from being unspiritual, assured that the spiritual priority of the Word would be maintained with proper care and discipline.

Two of the early church fathers, Chrysostom and Tertullian, testify to the significant ministry of the wives of elders and deacons. Not only did these women help maintain important family relations as models for the church, but they were ministers to the church along with their husbands. Gender did not seem to be a spiritual issue; equality was assumed (Galatians 3:28). Wives shared ministry with their husbands because marriage had united them not only in body but in spirit. This is implied by Paul when he asks: "Don't we have the right to take a believing wife along with us, as do the other apostles and the Lord's brothers and Cephas?" (1 Corinthians 9:5). Apparently the custom of the other apostles was to team up with their wives in ministry. Paul's singleness does not seem to have been the norm among the apostles.

That Paul should especially mention Cephas—Peter—is significant in light of Peter's admonition in one of his own letters:

> *Wives, in the same way be submissive to your husbands so that, if any of them do not believe the word, they may be won over without words by the behavior of their wives, when they see the purity and reverence of your lives.*
> (1 Peter 3:1–2)

Wives should not let outward adornment detract from their beauty of character (3:3–4). Nor should they attempt to domineer. Husbands, for their part, should "be considerate" and treat their wives "with respect" (3:7). Peter, too, recognized that the gracious gift of marriage was to be on display in the leadership ministry of the church.

Marriage and the family are foundational to the church and to society. Paul describes the church as an attractive bride loved by Christ Jesus, the heavenly Bridegroom (Ephesians 5:29). Our present-day preoccupation with gender rights and authority are not a part of the New Testament. Authority is in Christ and the Word, and the husband's true reflection of that authority in character and position is shared with his wife.

Servanthood, unity, vision, and responsiveness to the divine imperative—these are the ingredients of effective spiritual leadership. The Lord speaks to the church corporately, gifts the church corporately and lives and acts through the church corporately to cause the church to build itself up in love and reach out with that Calvary love to a lost, desperate world.

Shared vision comes not only from the preaching and teaching of God's Word but from the way it is fleshed out among the church's members, whose lives follow the model of dedicated, Spirit-filled leaders. Within every growing church is an enlarging circle of committed, accountable members who share the leaders' dedication to a divine imperative that embraces the ends of the earth.

Endnotes

[1]God's repeated command to Israel to "go to the place the Lord your God will choose as a dwelling place for his Name" (Deuteronomy 26:2; see also 12:11, 14; 16:15; 18:6; 31:11) leaves no doubt as to the importance, in God's sight, of such a central focus for His people, from which His glory and reputation would fan outward. In the New Testament, too, "beginning at Jerusalem" (Luke 24:44) suggests the same thought. The witness of the gospel should commence from Jerusalem and progress to "all Judea and Samaria, and to the ends of the earth" (Acts 1:8).

The "tongues of fire" which separated from a single fire and "came to rest on each" of the 120 assembled believers at Pentecost (Acts 2:3) are reminiscent of the pillar of fire that came upon the tabernacle in the desert whenever Israel encamped. In the desert it symbolized God's presence in mercy and grace (it rested over the Mercy Seat) amid His people.

When Jesus assured the Samaritan woman that rather than on Mt. Zion or Mt. Gerazim "the true worshipers will worship the Father in spirit and truth" (John 4:23), He was not disestablishing a locus for God's name where judgment (the cutting edge of truth) is meted out. Rather, He was predicting that the new locus would be *wherever* believers established a meeting place and *wherever* a gospel foundation was laid (see 1 Corinthians 3:10; 5:2–5). The universal church is always manifest in a particular place. At the same time, believers from various churches are tied by common bonds and share fellowship.

[2]Alliance constitutions (see *Manual of The Christian and Missionary Alliance*, U.S.A., 1989 edition, pp. 166–180, and Canadian edition, 88–97) distinguish between discipline for ordained clergy and lay members. This is predicated on the nature of their function, not on the nature of their importance. The sacred duty of representing the church in leadership implies not only preserving the primacy and authority of God's Word but also maintaining the unity of the church.

[3]I do not present "pastors and teachers" as separate roles but as dual roles. The two words are loaded with Old Testament meaning, particularly in the prophecies of Jeremiah, Ezekiel and Zechariah—prophecies that carry over into the gospels. Through the ministry of the Word in teaching, pastors have their main function. Peter exhorted elders to be "shepherds of God's flock that is under your care, serving as overseers" (1 Peter 5:2) until "the Chief Shepherd appears" (5:4). No doubt Peter recalled Jesus' discourse on the Good Shepherd (John 10:1–18), whose voice herds the flock with watchful care. For sure he remembered Jesus' post-resurrection words to him: "Feed my lambs," "Take care of my sheep," "Feed my sheep" (John 21:15–17). A pastor-teacher is primarily a feeder and a facilitator.

While Ephesians 4:11 is the only New Testament reference to pastor-teachers as congregational leaders, a similar association was made by Paul to the Ephesian elders (Acts 20:17–35). Paul climaxed his exhortation to them regarding their shepherding with these words: "Now I commit you to God and to the word of his grace, which can build you up and give you an inheritance among all those who are sanctified" (20:32). The discipline of the Word is a foremost need of elders, but their ministry of the Word is to give them "an inheritance among all those who are sanctified" (see also 2 Thessalonians 3:1; Colossians 1:3–8).

[4]Local Christian and Missionary Alliance churches in the United States have flexibility in constituting their Governing Board. Each church in its bylaws shall "(1) Determine the maximum number of Governing Board Members. (2) Specify the number of pastors, elders and deacons to serve on the Governing Board. (3) Designate other Governing Board members as the church may decide to elect" (*Manual* [1989 edition], p. 51). In Canada, the Governing Board is the Board of Elders, and deacons and deaconesses are designated as assistants.

Rigidity of government was not an objective in the New Testament church. Rather, spiritual trustworthiness was the standard, and the church looked to God to provide it with mature leaders. The New Testament pattern for church governance was apparently elders, with deacons and deaconesses as assistants to the elders. This reflected the primacy of the Word and the holiness of a unified, worshipful service within the church.

10

Proclamation and the Church

*I*n the prologue to his gospel, John unveils the incarnate Jesus as the church's proclamation, the Word:

> *In the beginning was the Word, and the Word was with God, and the Word was God. He was with God in the beginning. . . . He was in the world, and though the world was made through him, the world did not recognize him. . . . Yet to all who received him, to those who believed in his name, he gave the right to become children of God. . . . The Word became flesh and made his dwelling among us.*
> (John 1:1–14)

187

In Acts, Luke depicts church growth in similar terminology:

> *The Word of God spread. The number of disciples in Jerusalem increased rapidly, and a large number of priests became obedient to the faith.*
> (Acts 6:7)

> *The Word of God continued to increase and spread.*
> (12:24)

> *The Word of the Lord spread widely and grew in power.*
> (19:20)

Throughout the New Testament this interchange of the *Word, Christ* and the *church* is striking. They are one divine proclamation. Paul writes to the church at Thessalonica: "We also thank God continually because, when you received the Word of God, which you heard from us, you accepted it . . . as it actually is, the Word of God, which is at work in you who believe" (1 Thessalonians 2:13).

As the Word is believed in reality and truth, the proclamation of it is transmitted similarly to new locations. Paul goes on to say to the Thessalonians: "You, brothers, became imitators of God's churches in Judea, which are in Christ Jesus" (2:14). When the Word is faithfully preached and received in faith by those who hear it, this transmittal pattern repeats itself.

The awesome mystery of proclamation is this: As believers receive the Word of God, they embrace as well Christ and His body, the church. The church is not only known as the body of Christ (1 Corinthians 12:27) but also "the pillar and foundation of the truth" (1 Timothy 3:15). Pillars and foundations are substantive, authentic. So is the church. The church is the Word of God at work among its members; the combination is incarnate proclamation. James Daane has observed:

The current crisis of the pulpit is, therefore, a crisis of everything that is meant by "church." Why? Because a person's existence and function as a preacher, and the church's existence as "the pillar and ground of the truth" and function of proclaiming that truth, derive their distinctive reality and function from the nature of the Word. [1]

The Word and the Church

In the aftermath of the Reformation, Protestants considered the Word and its proclamation through preaching to be the heart and ministry of the church. The church recognized the Word of God as divine revelation designed to meet humankind's need for redemption. Short of redemption, a person could not live a fulfilled life upon earth or be ready for life hereafter. For the most part, Protestants looked upon the church as comprised of baptized members whose confession was expressed in Communion and whose discipline was maintained by church leaders.

Religion for these earlier Protestants was more dogma and community fellowship than the church itself or its programmed activity. Biological growth and the strength of the nuclear family sustained the church. Until the last half of the 19th century, programmed evangelism was practically unknown.

In today's cosmopolitan, mass media world, the local community has almost lost its identity. Neighbors are strangers, and family structure has little significance. No longer is biological growth a strong factor in the church's continuity. Neither does dogma determine the church's character. For many, the "electronic church" has become a comfortable substitute for "dressing up" and driving several miles to "their" church. The proliferation of parachurch organizations, each vying for money, encourages a consumer mindset and shallow church loyalty. Changes of this magnitude have profoundly altered the church's image, to the confusion of both the secular and Christian worlds.

Rather than to compare the church as it was with the church as it is, we need to understand the church as God intended it to be. The present-day sociological changes have come as no surprise to God. We may therefore assume that the genetic code He built into the church before its birth anticipated today's conditions and made provision for the church to overcome them.

In New Testament times, local churches were frontier launching pads for the gospel. In confronting both Judaism and the pagan world, New Testament churches had high profiles. The character and testimony of believers, expressed in corporate church life, were of greater force than the sermons the ministering elders preached. Believers were known as the people of the "Way" (see Acts 9:2; 19:9, 23). They impacted not only their local, ethnic communities but a cosmopolitan world as well. Paul tells the church in Corinth: "You show that you are a letter from Christ, the result of our ministry, written not with ink but with the Spirit of the living God, not on tablets of stone but on tablets of human hearts" (2 Corinthians 3:3).

Paul's reference in that comment to "the result of our ministry" was not boastfulness. Rather, it summarized the faithful transmission of the Word preached to people where they lived. That divine imperative ruling Paul's pastoral servanthood controlled the lives of believers and the life of the church as a body. Thus the Word and the church became a unified proclamation. Paul describes the churches at Thessalonica, Colosse and Ephesus in similar words. In Paul's eyes, this was the pattern for all churches, beginning with the church in Jerusalem (see Acts 26:19–20).

Proclamation Defined

To proclaim is to declare publicly what is solemn, official and formal to the corporate nature and function of a responsible body. The proclamation of the Word is more than pulpit preaching. It includes congregational demonstration through celebration, edification, witness and missions. Proclamation of the Word is made credible to a lost world through Christ's body, the church. The Word takes on "flesh" in order to be a glorious revelation among people. The church not only affirms truth, it becomes itself an established pillar of the truth. This reality was demonstrated in the Thessalonian church:

> We know, brothers loved by God, that he has chosen you, because our gospel came to you not simply with words, but also with power, with the Holy Spirit and with deep conviction. You know how we lived among you for your sake. You became imitators of us and of the Lord; in spite of severe suffering, you welcomed the message with the joy given by the Holy Spirit. And so you became a model to all the believers in Macedonia and Achaia. The Lord's message rang out from you not only in Macedonia and Achaia—your faith in God has become known everywhere.
>
> (1 Thessalonians 1:4–8)

This transformation of the Word into dynamic flesh is the core-factor of the church. It is not the Word in an outlined agenda or in programmed speeches. It is the Word of truth in flesh-and-blood people. This is what gives the church its credibility. Faith, love and hope are to be demonstrated, just as they were at Colosse. Paul tells the Colossians he always thanks God when he prays for them

> . . . because we have heard of your faith in Christ Jesus and of the love you have for all the saints—the faith and love that spring from the hope that is stored up for you in heaven and that you have already heard about in the word of truth, the gospel that has come to you. All over the world this gospel is bearing fruit and growing, just as it has been doing among you since the day you heard it and

understood God's grace in all its truth.
(Colossians 1:4–6)

That the church would embody these qualities was one of Jesus' petitions in His high priestly prayer:

"My prayer is not for [the 12 disciples] alone. I pray also for those who will believe in me through their message, that all of them may be one, Father, just as you are in me and I am in you. May they also be in us so that the world may believe that you have sent me."
(John 17:20–21)

The Word fleshed out in body-life is the means God has ordained to reach the world with the good news of Jesus Christ.

In tracing biblical history we realize that the church as a divine community is not one alternative among others; it is at the very heart of God's call. The unifying power of the message believed has an expansive outreach also. The Word and the church cannot be separated. Preaching and teaching are central to unifying faith and the life of the church. What is believed in togetherness will be expressed in body-life.

The Preaching of the Word and the Church

The preaching of the Word in the assembly of saints allows an expression of unity in truth and Spirit. The Holy Spirit, illuminating the Word preached by his appointed servants, elicits from the gathered church mutual faith in the authority of Christ and His Word. The Word in turn is affirmed by obedience of faith expressed publicly in unity.

The Sunday school and home Bible studies, valuable as they are, cannot take the place of the preaching of the Word to the gathered assembly. That preaching is crucial to the very nature and function of the church. But preaching without a context for corporate proclamation is merely sermonizing.

For the gathered believers to receive and assimilate the Word so as to own it as their own proclamation, several elements are vital, specifically: celebration, edification, evangelization, missions and intercession.

Celebration

Celebration figured prominently in Israel's national life. The spectacular deliverance God granted the nation at the Red Sea called for celebration and praise to God (Exodus 15:1–18). The annual festivals—Passover, Firstfruits, Pentecost, Trumpets, Atonement, Tabernacles (Leviticus 23)— were national convocations of celebration. Jericho's walls tumbled as the children of Israel raised their victory shout to God (Joshua 6:16, 20). The Lord fought for Israel "as they began to sing and praise" (2 Chronicles 20:22). Many of the Psalms were especially composed for Israel's gatherings in celebration of God's mercy and mighty power in behalf of His people. In King Hezekiah's day, as the renovated Temple was purified for reuse, Hezekiah

> . . . stationed the Levites in the temple of the LORD with cymbals, harps and lyres in the way prescribed by David and Gad the king's seer and Nathan the prophet; this was commanded by the LORD through his prophets. . . . As the offering began, singing to the LORD began also, accompanied by trumpets and the instruments of David king of Israel. The whole assembly bowed in worship, while the singers sang and the trumpeters played. . . .
>
> When the offerings were finished, the king and everyone present with him knelt down and worshiped. King Hezekiah and his officials ordered the Levites to praise the LORD with the words of David and of Asaph the seer. So they sang praises with gladness and bowed their heads and worshiped.
>
> (2 Chronicles 29:25–30)

Celebration is an important element in the proclamation of the church. Worship is personal, but it is also to be a formal and public confession of God's character and faithfulness, of Christ's worth and fullness, of the Holy Spirit's ministry in presence and power among God's gathered people. A celebration of the Word as God's revelation is important preparation to worshipful service and body-life proclamation.

An invocation, the Gloria Patri and an appropriate Bible text have become standard and familiar introductions to the worship hour. Corporate singing and prayer attune our minds and hearts to God.

The poetic language of song tailors it to worship. Pitch, rhythm, duration, color, form and message can convey in worship exaltation, adoration and truth in conformity with God's Word. Gustav Oehler, in *Theology of the Old Testament,* wrote in 1883: "There is so close a connection between sacred song and prophecy that the former is itself called prophesying (1 Chronicles 25:2ff.), and the chief singers appointed by David (1 Chronicles 15:1, 5; 2 Chronicles 29:30; 35:15) are called prophets and seers."[2]

Music's rich diversity provides us with choices appropriate to the occasion and purpose of our service to the Lord. In worship, believers intend for God's worthiness to be celebrated with honest motive.

In our music-making (and our praying), Paul exhorts a balance between ecstasy and discipline. We worship with the understanding of our minds as well as with the passion of our spirits (1 Corinthians 14:16). He encourages the Ephesians to address one another "with psalms, hymns and spiritual songs." He continues: "Sing and make music in your hearts to the Lord, always giving thanks to God the Father for everything, in the name of our Lord Jesus Christ" (Ephesians 5:19–20).

The Music of Celebration as a Teacher

We too quickly overlook singing as a method of teaching and admonishing one another. Paul encourages the Colossians to "let the word of Christ dwell in you richly . . . as you sing psalms, hymns and spiritual songs with gratitude in your hearts to God" (Colossians 3:16). Hymns, by definition, are a form of direct address to God; songs are a form of testimony and witness to others. Both are needed. Spiritual singing is a significant form of participation in the body-life of the church. It can create an environment for worship. It is spiritual preparation for the Word of God preached.

Hymns are important to the church's proclamation. Martin Luther has been called the father of congregational singing, and singing largely solidified the Reformation movement. John Wesley had the gift of preaching. His brother Charles had the gift of song-writing. John's sermons are largely forgotten, but who can forget Charles' hymns? Through singing the church recalls its heritage of faith, its message of truth and its motive of service. Above all, worshipful music exalts our Triune God in unity of voice.

If we are not careful, these primary values of church music can be sacrificed to the whims and tastes of people saturated by an adulterated culture. To sing merely for psychological and emotional effect may be enjoyable, but it does not maximize the potential God created it for. Sacred music is intended for the worship and praise of God and as a testimony to God's great grace. If at the same time it is enjoyable, that is a byproduct. There is a place in our singing for solemn, deep, heart-searching prayer and confession; there is also a place for victorious, ringing testimony. Music must be used intelligently and with careful preparation. For this reason many denominations produce their own hymnals and train their own musicians. A church hymnal is designed to unite a congregation around a legacy of faith and fellowship.[3]

A.B. Simpson composed many poems and songs. Some 162 of these were published, although far fewer currently are in print. They have had a lasting and profound effect on the theology and outreach of The Christian and Missionary Alliance that he founded. Today Simpson's songs still form an ecclesiastical legacy. A.W. Tozer has commented:

> When the facts are all known, it will be found that The Christian and Missionary Alliance owes nearly as much to its hymns as it does to its preaching. The hymns of Dr. Simpson, considered as literature, may not be classed with some of the great hymns of the Church, but they have given doctrinal direction to the movement and wings to its missionary zeal.[4]

Divine Providence placed a hymnal in the middle of the Bible. Psalm 119, the longest song and the lengthiest chapter in the Bible, is entirely a celebration of the Word of God. Many of our present-day hymns are prayers, some are confessions of faith, others speak of God's attributes. The hymnal is second only to the Bible in its provision of spiritual truth and inspiration, whether in the corporate assembly or in private devotional use. Both in moments of spiritual need and in times of inner praise, the Spirit frequently prompts a familiar hymn or song. Hymns and songs that have survived a long pilgrimage with depth, theological truth and dignity are reminders of the church's own validity.

Edification

If a local church is to proclaim convincingly the majesty of God and the Good News of a Savior, its members must be able to "give the reason for the hope that [they] have" (1 Peter 3:15). Edification—the building, establishing, strengthening of the church body—is therefore another key element in proclamation. Some of the building up comes through celebration, as we have observed. Other vital aspects of edification occur in teaching and training sessions, in home Bible studies and prayer meetings. These cultivate involvement, mostly in small groups. But the Bible's best sanctioned method of edification is the public reading and preaching of the Word of God as the church is assembled for worship.

The reading of God's Word traditionally has been a central feature of public worship, dating back to the post-exilic synagogues. At least by New Testament times, the Scriptures were first read in Hebrew, then in the Aramaic paraphrase known as the Targum. These readings were followed by a homily explaining and applying the Word.

On a visit to His home town, Jesus, "as was his custom" (Luke 4:16), attended the Nazareth synagogue on the Sabbath. He stood up and read a portion of Isaiah 61. When He had finished, He "rolled up the scroll" (4:20), returned it to the attendant and sat down. The scrolls had a sacred receptacle and were carefully guarded by the attendant. The people riveted their attention on Jesus, waiting for the homily. Luke does not record the extent of Jesus' remarks, but he tells us that Jesus did not fail to make the application: "Today this scripture is fulfilled in your hearing" (4:21). Luke also reports that the people "were amazed at the gracious words that came from his lips" (4:22).

The same format was customary at the synagogue in Antioch, Pisidia, where Paul and Barnabas, on their first mission, stopped to worship. After the reading from the Law and the Prophets, the synagogue ruler sent word, "If you have a message of encouragement for the people, please speak" (Acts 13:15). Paul's message follows in the next 26 verses of Acts 13. But note that the public reading of the Scriptures held precedence, and the spoken message was an explanation of the authoritative Word of God.

This practice continued in the early church. Justin Martyr, in *The First Apology,* a book that dates back to A.D. 150, describes the typical Sunday worship service in Rome as mostly reading the memoirs of the apostles and the writings of the prophets "as long as time permits." When the reader was finished, the president would speak, admonishing and exhorting the people to follow the noble teaching and the examples of the holy men who had written.[5]

Jesus placed great value on the Scriptures. Tempted by Satan, He each time responded with Scripture (Matthew 4:1–10). He said to His disciples, "Do not think that I have come to abolish the Law or the Prophets; I have not come to abolish them but to fulfill them" (Matthew 5:17). On Resurrection Day evening, the discouraged couple who suddenly learned the identity of the Stranger who had walked to Emmaus with them, commented to each other: "Were not our hearts burning within us while he talked with us on the road and opened the Scriptures to us?" (Luke 24:32). Later when Jesus appeared to His own disciples, Luke quotes Him saying: "Everything must be fulfilled that is written about me in the Law of Moses, the Prophets and the Psalms" (24:44). Luke adds: "He opened their minds so they could understand the Scriptures" (24:45). Jesus found within those Old Testament Scriptures predictions of His suffering, death and—three days later—resurrection. He found that repentance and forgiveness of sins would be preached in His name to all nations (24:46–47). Jesus used the Scriptures comprehensively. He saw them as a canon of fixed truth.

Preaching as Edification

Explicit faith in the authoritative Word is required of the church for its ministry of proclamation. The Bible represents itself as the objective Word of God, the whole counsel of God, and a complete and final revelation for faith and practice. Unless the Word is preached as truth revealed, unless it opens the hearts of people to see revealed truth for themselves, unless this truth is applied as God's truth and not merely the words of humankind, preaching falls short. As Ray Petry has observed:

> The Christian road to God has always been in united pilgrimage of "Word and Worship." This the early church felt in a great blaze of intercommunion. This

was the passionate witness to the living Christ and the reverent obeisance to the divine purpose that made Christianity real—whenever it was real—in the first fifteen hundred years of its history. This the Luthers, the Calvins and the Wesleys discovered and reapplied.[6]

The Bible presents the sovereign call of God to the ministry of the Word as a personal call that is affirmed through the church. The principle of divine selectivity is neither a casual happening nor a self-appointment. The uniqueness of the call of God and the solemnity of the position is because it is to the ministry of the all-important Word. This is a lifetime call. Prayer and the ministry of the Word are its dual priorities.

Paul's preaching confidence was in the Word, and his confidence for the future of the church was in God and the Word of His grace preached by ministers who were servants of that Word. Paul charged Timothy, whom he mentored in the ministry: "Preach the Word; be prepared in season and out of season; correct, rebuke and encourage—with great patience and careful instruction" (2 Timothy 4:2).

Preaching for the edification of the church is fundamental to the life of the church and for the proclamation of the gospel. The spiritual health of the corporate church requires a balanced diet. The will of God as a divine imperative comes from the whole counsel of God.

The Word must be presented in the way it ought to be heard—with decisiveness, strength and courage of faith, with contrition and self-consecration. The purpose of the Word is to reveal the God of the Word, and until people meet God they will not experience the truth being taught. The church that fails to experience the truth it is taught will fail as a witness to the world.

Evangelization

The third element of the church's proclamation is evangelization. Jesus Christ came into the world to seek and to save sinners (1 Timothy 1:15). The church must seek out those who need to be reached.

As we had occasion to note earlier, the church at Thessalonica became a model of evangelism. "The Lord's message rang out" from them; their faith in God became known everywhere (1 Thessalonians 1:7–8). When it came to the gospel, the Thessalonian believers were enthusiasts! Their very lives were such a powerful proclamation of the gospel that it became known all over the area. The free course of the gospel begins with a sanctified local church. To strategize evangelism without the support of spiritual body-life will produce hollow results.

Evangelism fails when it is regarded as a special activity for special people at special times. It also fails when the church's obligation to *world* evangelization remains unfulfilled. Believers within the church are "saints" not by virtue of their good deeds but by the grace of God. As recipients of His grace, they have a disciple-making responsibility in "all nations."

The need of a home base in cross-cultural ministry is readily recognized. Not as easily recognized is the need of a home base in evangelism at home. Sanctification and the filling of the Holy Spirit are vital to effective missionary service. They are just as vital for evangelism.

The church as "the pillar and foundation of the truth" is ordained to affirm the gospel and to demonstrate its validity. God gives the church evangelists as a special appointment to announce the gospel to those who have not believed, but the whole corporate church is to support evangelism by its witness. This proclamation is in both word and deed. The church as a whole prepares the soil, sows the seed and waters the ground with prayer and good deeds.

God designed the church as a marvelous representation of the power of the gospel. In the church people of different vocations, backgrounds, abilities, ages, capacities and race are made "one" in Christ Jesus. Paul commends the Colossian church for its faith in Christ and its love for all the saints. He rejoices that the gospel, which he refers to as "the word of truth" has reached them. Then he talks about the gospel:

> All over the world this gospel is bearing fruit and growing, just as it has been doing among you since the day you heard it and understood God's grace in all its truth. You learned it from Epaphras, our dear fellow servant, who is a faithful minister of Christ on our behalf, and who also told us of your love in the Spirit.
> (Colossians 1:6–8)

Paul says the gospel became effective as new believers came to understand *God's grace in all its truth.* This grace of God was exemplified by love—an infectious truth caught from their evangelist-leader, Epaphras. The gospel becomes most evident in the love of God's people for each other. Such love is explosive. It reaches out "all over the world," producing fruit beyond the local church.

Missions

Salvation is neither earned nor deserved. The marvel of God's grace, manifested by love in the church, makes believers debtors to the whole human race. Simpson expressed it in verse:

> We all are debtors to our race;
>   God holds us bound to one another;
> The gifts and blessings of His grace
>   Were given thee to give our brother.

Jesus Christ, the living reigning Savior, died for our sins, rose again for our justification and now commands everyone to repent. Those who, in contrition, turn to Him for forgiveness become by faith His children—new creations in Christ Jesus.

Missions is not an appendage to the church's life but a continuum of its very nature. Jesus Christ is Savior for the whole world. The gospel is universal and anticipates a church comprised of every nation, tribe and tongue. Jesus said, "This gospel of the kingdom will be preached to the whole world as a testimony to all nations, and then the end will come" (Matthew 24:14). He commanded His followers to "make disciples of all nations" (28:19). Missions, far from detracting from evangelism, adds an important dimension to it. World evangelization plants churches among unreached peoples, and as new frontiers are added to the church, the hope of Christ's personal return brightens.

Local churches need such a world vision. Jesus urged His disciples: "Open your eyes and look at the fields! They are ripe for harvest" (John 4:35). As then, so now, people catch the vision of harvest only as leaders point the way. Robert Hall Glover, Alliance missionary to China and, from 1913 to 1921, director of Alliance missions worldwide, put it well:

> There is undoubted truth in the old saying, "Like pastor, like people." Christians as a rule do not go beyond their leaders, whether in knowledge, zeal, consecration or sacrifice. But they are usually ready— at least a goodly proportion of them—to follow a leader. The pastor more than any other individual, . . . has the opportunity of influencing missionary recruiting, praying and giving. But that influence will be exerted, and effective, only in the measure in which he himself has caught the missionary vision, has squarely faced the question whether he ought to be a foreign missionary, has a clear conviction of a divine call to the home pastorate and conceives of that position as designed for the inspiring and leading forward of his

flock to assume fully their rightful part in the carrying out of Christ's great missionary purpose and program.[7]

Intercession

Prayer is essential to every aspect of church life and ministry. But the church in corporate prayer is a special dimension of church life. "The family that prays together stays together" is true of the church, too. God's house is to be a house of prayer (Isaiah 56:7; Matthew 21:13). Prayer cells, Bible study and prayer groups, Sunday school classes and youth meetings that incorporate prayer are all commendable. But prayer takes on a whole new dimension when the corporate church gathers to pray. There the church as a spiritual body senses its spiritual heartbeat and its burden of need.

In the early church prayer was no minor ingredient of the church's life and ministry. Before Pentecost, in the Jerusalem upper room, the disciples and others "joined together constantly in prayer" (Acts 1:14). Following Pentecost, all of those brought into the church devoted themselves "to the apostles' teaching and to the fellowship, to the breaking of bread and to prayer" (2:42). Peter and John were on their way to the temple for the three o'clock "time of prayer" when they met the lame man at the temple gate (3:1–2). And when the disciples faced critical problems, they gave themselves to earnest intercession (4:23–30).

The apostles made prayer and the ministry of the Word their overriding priorities (Acts 6:4). At the very time "many people had gathered and were praying," God miraculously released Peter from prison (12:12). It was while the church staff at Antioch was fasting and praying that God called Paul and Barnabas to be the church's two first missionaries (13:1–3).

Exhortations to prayer abound in the Letters: Paul urges the Colossian believers: "Devote yourselves to prayer, being watchful and thankful" (Colossians 4:2). He requests the Colossians to pray for him and his coworkers "that God may open a door for our message, so that we may proclaim the mystery of Christ, for which I am in chains. Pray that I may proclaim it clearly, as I should" (4:3–4). To the Ephesians he writes: "And pray in the Spirit on all occasions with all kinds of prayers and requests. With this in mind, be alert and always keep on praying for all the saints" (Ephesians 6:18). "Be . . . faithful in prayer," he tells the Christians in Rome. He urges Timothy, his protégé in the ministry, to see, "first of all, that requests, prayers, intercession and thanksgiving be made for everyone" (1 Timothy 2:1).

From the writings of the early church fathers, we know that it was customary for the pastor-leader, during worship, to lead the gathered believers in prayer—a custom that largely continues yet today. The corporate church needs to hear the pastor voicing in prayer the needs of the congregation and the burdens of his own heart for the church. The 12 disciples heard Jesus praying thus, and they asked Him to teach them to pray. Genuine prayer is both effective and instructive.

The church has a powerful message to proclaim. Its message is proclaimed through five functions: worship, edification, witness, missions and prayer. Almost everything a church does (or should do) may be classified under those five functions. Each is distinctive. Each deserves recognition. How well they are balanced, integrated and implemented depends largely on the quality of the church's leaders.

God has no second-rate standards. Leaders may be satisfied with modest success; Christ is not. When He designed His New Testament church, He intended it to see great success. Through prayer and the ministry of the Word, God transmits His values to the church. The church's health curve follows the strength of the pulpit; preaching and praying are at the heart of church life. The receptivity and obedience with which the congregation receives the

Word preached will largely determine how clearly the church's proclamation "rings out" to the watching world.

Endnotes

[1] James Daane, *Preaching with Confidence* (Grand Rapids: Wm. B. Eerdmans Publishing Co., 1980), p. 7.

[2] Gustave Oehler, *Theology of the Old Testament* (Grand Rapids: Zondervan Publishing House, n.d.), p. 367. This is a revision of the translation appearing in Clark's Foreign Theological Library together with an introduction and notes by George E. Day.

[3] The Alliance to date has published eight hymnals: 1891, 1897, 1904, 1908, 1936, 1962, 1978 and 1992. Eugene Rivard in his 1991 doctoral dissertation, "The Hymnody of The Christian and Missionary Alliance (1891–1978) as a Reflection of its Theology and Development," (Southwestern Baptist Theological Seminary, Fort Worth, Texas) has made a significant contribution to our knowledge and understanding of Alliance hymnody. An earlier dissertation by Alton Bynum, completed at New Orleans Baptist Theological Seminary in 1975, analyzes the "Music Program and Practices of The Christian and Missionary Alliance." Bynum makes this comment: "Since so many of the hymns of The C&MA were written by Simpson and those associated with him, it was perhaps inevitable that they should demonstrate the doctrinal bias or emphasis of the denomination, and indeed may have been calculated to do so. Of the 426 hymns by the authors and composers previously mentioned, 250 of them gave expression to at least one of the 'fourfold gospel' doctrines, or to Christian service and missions" (p.79).

[4] A.W. Tozer, "Have You Ever Sung a Hymn?" *The Alliance Weekly* (January 22, 1938), p. 51.

[5] Justin Martyrs' "First Apology," *The Ante-Nicene Fathers*, Vol. 1 (Grand Rapids: Wm. B. Eerdmans Publishing Co., 1953), p. cvii.

[6] Ray C. Petry, *Preaching in the Great Tradition* (Philadelphia: Westminster Press, 1950), p. 96.

[7] Robert Hall Glover, *The Bible Basis of Missions* (Los Angeles: Bible House of Los Angeles, 1946), p. 4.

11

The Church:
In Christ's Image

*T*he climactic event of world history is the return of Jesus Christ to receive His bride, the church. Paul assures us that even now Christ is preparing His church "to present her to himself as a radiant church, without . . . blemish, but holy and blameless" (Ephesians 5:27).

There are parallels between this present era of preparation for the church and Jesus' preparation for the perfection of His earthly life and the fulfillment of His earthly ministry. Jesus sensed His dependence on God the Father: "The Son can do nothing by himself; he can do only what he sees his Father doing, because whatever the Father does the Son also does" (John 5:19). And again, "By myself I can do nothing; . . . I seek not to please myself but him who sent me" (5:30). The church likewise is dependent. It is dependent on Jesus, its Lord and Head. As Jesus sought to please God, so the church seeks to please Christ Jesus.

Jesus dispelled any possible delusions of self-sufficiency the church might have when He declared to His apostles just before His death: "I am the vine; you are the branches. If a man remains in me and I in him, he will bear much fruit; apart from me you can do nothing" (John 15:5). Nothing. Nothing.

Jesus, lifted up by both the cross and the resurrection, taught His disciples the enabling relationship-presence He was providing in order for them to bear much fruit. Jesus' Great Commission was an announcement, an order and a promise:

> *"All authority in heaven and on earth has been given to me. Therefore go and make disciples of all nations, baptizing them in the name of the Father and of the Son and of the Holy Spirit, and teaching them to obey everything I have commanded you. And surely I am with you always, to the very end of the age."*
> (Matthew 28:18–20)

Christ Is the Key to Christlikeness

Christ's continued presence was the result of Pentecost and the descent of His Holy Spirit to indwell the newly born church. In a sermon preached in 1887 just prior to the organization of The International Alliance, A.B. Simpson chose as his subject, "The Secret of the Christian Life." His text was from Philippians:

> *I am not saying this because I am in need, for I have learned to be content whatever the circumstances. I know what it is to be in need, and I know what it is to have plenty. I have learned the secret of being content in any*

and every situation, whether well fed or hungry, whether
living in plenty or in want. I can do everything through
him who gives me strength.
                              (Philippians 4:11–13)

As Simpson delivered his sermon, the vision of a missionary people united for a worldwide ministry in dependence upon the indwelling Christ was the foundation of what a decade later would be called The Christian and Missionary Alliance. Simpson stressed the personal secret that Paul had discovered for living the Christian life:

> It is not ideas, or principles of truth, but [the secret] is a Person. The letter to the Colossians tells us what it is. This secret is the mystery which has been hidden from ages and generations, but now is made manifest to His saints: Christ in you, the hope of glory. It is an open secret, one which everybody can understand. "I can do everything through [Christ] who gives me strength." That is the secret that Paul learned. It went with him down into the Adriatic, and up in the mountainous region of Colosse; it went with him to the dungeon and down into the grave, and it will appear with him at the judgment—Christ in him, the hope of glory. [1]

The Christlikeness of the church and the fulfillment of the Great Commission are made possible by Christ Himself through His indwelling Spirit. The soul of The Christian and Missionary Alliance was established on this foundation truth. Christ was indwelt by the Father through the Spirit. The church indwelt by Christ through His Spirit. The ministry Jesus had on earth in relationship with the Father is the ministry the church is to have on earth in relationship with Christ. To make the church in the likeness of Jesus Christ is God's main goal in this age. Not so surprising, considering the relational parallels, we discover certain similarities between the church and the life Jesus lived on earth.

Christlike in its Faith in God's Word

The church is Christlike in its faith in God's Word. Matthew's Gospel is a link between Judaism and Christianity, characterized by the phrase, "that it might be fulfilled." God the Father fulfilled His Word in Jesus' life. Inasmuch as Jesus *was* the Word enfleshed (John 1:14), there was nothing perfunctory about Jesus' fulfilling the Word. As a 12-year-old boy, Jesus was discovered "in the temple courts, sitting among the teachers, listening to them and asking them questions" (Luke 2:46). Nor was it totally a learning experience for Jesus: "Everyone who heard him was amazed at his understanding and his answers" (2:47). As we saw earlier, Jesus overcame Satan through His faith in God's Word. He told the people of Nazareth, His home town, that He was the fulfillment of Isaiah 61:1–2 (Luke 4:16–21).

The church exists to proclaim God's Word and to demonstrate it as the authoritative Word of God. The Hebrew term for "word" is *dabar*, meaning "event." When it is understood as truth and true to reality, this "event" produces conviction and, ultimately, judgment. It fulfills God's purpose. The Word never attempts to curry people's favor; rather, it points them directly to the grace and power of God. It is sin-annulling, life-changing, death-defeating, creative, healing, powerful and dynamic. The Word of God and the worship of God are central to the life of the church.

One of the great barriers to the gospel is the institutional church that glosses the gospel, failing to demonstrate its truthfulness. The great potential of the gospel comes when the church becomes convinced that it is God's vehicle for evangelism and missions and acts accordingly.

The preaching of the Word, when integrated with body-life proclamation, is the functional base for evangelism and missions. Biblical evangelism in full function is church-centered evangelism. The same may be said for missions. To those He sent to announce the coming kingdom Jesus declared: "He who listens to you listens to me; he who rejects you rejects me; but he who rejects me rejects him who sent me" (Luke 10:16). The divine Word, enfleshed by those who minister, becomes a witness that demands a response. When those who hear the Word receive it—enflesh it—in obedience, it continues its dynamic mission.

Over and over in his letters, Paul gives thanks to God for local churches (Romans 1:8; 1 Corinthians 1:4–5; Ephesians 1:15–16; Philippians 1:3–5; Colossians 1:3–4; 1 Thessalonians 1:2–3) Each time, his thanksgiving focuses on the proclamation of faith produced when the Word was preached and received. God says through Isaiah:

> As the rain and the snow
>   come down from heaven,
> and do not return to it
>   without watering the earth
> and making it bud and flourish,
>   so that it yields seed for the sower and bread for
>   the eater,
> so is my word that goes out from my mouth:
>   it will not return to me empty,
> but will accomplish what I desire
>   and achieve the purpose for which I sent it.
>   (Isaiah 55:10–11)

The Word of God is "living and active. Sharper than any double-edged sword, it penetrates even to dividing soul and spirit, joints and marrow; it judges the thoughts and attitudes of the heart" (Hebrews 4:12). The sword's two edges are final judgment and the saving grace of the atonement. Hosts of sinners believed this and acted upon it, forming the New Testament churches we find in Acts and the letters (and countless others founded through the ministry of the other apostles). The church exists to be the Word made flesh and to dwell among men, that men might behold the glory of God's one and only Son, who came from the Father, full of grace and truth. The church is Christlike in its faith in God's Word. It manifests Jesus Christ, the living Word even as Jesus Christ manifested the Father by fulfilling the divine written Word.

Christlike in its Service and Purpose

"My food," Jesus told His disciples as they rejoined Him at the Sychar well, "is to do the will of him who sent me and to finish his work. Do you not say, 'Four months more and then the harvest'? I tell you, open your eyes and look at the fields! They are ripe for harvest" (John 4:34–35). Jesus voluntarily entered into His Father's work and chose disciples who should enter into the work with Him. The church's "food" is in its fellowship of service, nurtured in God's will and purpose. Worship in the truth of God's Word forms a fellowship, and that fellowship, nurtured in God's will and purpose, motivates service— the central core and nature of the church.

Jesus announced the kingdom of God to a company of 12 disciples:

> *Jesus went up on a mountainside and called to him those he wanted, and they came to him. He appointed twelve— designating them apostles—that they might be with him and that he might send them out to preach and to have authority to drive out demons.*
> (Mark 3:13–15)

In the Old Testament, the number 12 carries metaphorical significance, being linked with the elective purposes of God.² Jesus chose the Twelve to be with Him and to become disciples for the work of God's kingdom.

The whole church is built to be a fellowship of service, modeled after the pattern of its leaders. The whole church is called a temple and so is each local church. Paul distinguishes between the church as a whole and the local church in some of his remarks to the Ephesians: "In [Christ] the whole building is joined together and rises to become a holy temple in the Lord. And in him you [believers at Ephesus] too are being built together to become a dwelling in which God lives by his Spirit" (Ephesians 2:21–22).

The church is also called God's "house," and Paul describes the church at Ephesus to Timothy as God's "household": "If I am delayed, you will know how people ought to conduct themselves in God's household, which is the church of the living God, the pillar and foundation of the truth" (1 Timothy 3:15; see also 1:3). As the home is foundational to society, so the church is foundational to the kingdom.

A distinct behavioral pattern of family living should characterize the church to express the kingdom and its King. Explicitly, the local church is a place of holiness. The purpose for the church's existence demands that it should be kept holy for the presence of God. His "eyes are too pure to look on evil" (Habakkuk 1:13). The church that does not pursue and maintain holiness as a clear objective need not expect to experience God's presence.

Driving out the forces of evil and disciplining the church are both necessary. Building the church is a process of fitting the "stones" together for greatest stability and strength. Peter says, "You also, like living stones, are being built into a spiritual house to be a holy priesthood, offering spiritual sacrifices acceptable to God through Jesus Christ" (1 Peter 2:5). If believers are the living stones, holiness is the "mortar" that cements the temple.

The Process Includes Church Discipline

Consistent with maintaining holiness, Paul instructed the church at Corinth to "put away the wicked man" who had defiled God's house with his sexual immorality (1 Corinthians 5:13; see entire chapter). Sin left unjudged or unchecked clouds the image of Christ and hinders the proclamation of the Word.

Church discipline, when properly applied, is a powerful message. The blatant dishonesty of Ananias and Sapphira (Acts 5:1–11), the disruptions caused by idle busybodies (2 Thessalonians 3:11–12), the unscriptural teaching of legalists (Galatians 1:6–9), the hollow and deceptive philosophy of teachers who captivate unsuspecting members (Colossians 2:8), the corrupting influence of Hymenaeus and Alexander (1 Timothy 5:19–20).

The instances just cited are of gross sin publicly known. Paul instructed Titus to encourage sound doctrine. The mouths of those who oppose it must be stopped. Even in the early church there were rebellious people, mere talkers and deceivers seeking dishonest gain. Titus was to rebuke sharply the careless and unspiritual members who gave ear to these opposers. It is a tough assignment, but it is very necessary to the church's health and to its reflection of the image of Christ Jesus.

When church discipline is called for, leaders should have two objectives in view: to purify the church, thus strengthening its proclamation of Jesus Christ, and to restore the offender or offenders. Unless leaders are grounded in God's Word and represent a fellowship nurtured in God's will and purpose, the exercise of discipline can create more problems that it solves. Church leaders dare not exercise discipline unprepared and ill-equipped.

God has given the church gifts of spiritual leadership "to prepare God's people for works of service" (Ephesians 4:12). These services are calculated to build up the church, fostering unity in the faith and in the knowledge of Jesus Christ. The ultimate objective: full Christlikeness (4:13). So lofty an objective may at times seem unrealistic, but the Scriptures leave us no room for options.

The church must "reach"—persist—toward these objectives. Through Christ's presence and enabling, the church despite its internal faults can triumph. Without this dominant spirit of faith, church discipline will seldom prove successful.

On the other hand, if discipline is supported by unity in the faith, maturity of knowledge and a vision for Christ's fullness,

> . . . then we will no longer be infants, tossed back and forth by the waves, and blown here and there by every wind of teaching and by the cunning and craftiness of men in their deceitful scheming. Instead, speaking the truth in love, we will in all things grow up into him who is the Head, that is, Christ. From him the whole body, joined and held together by every supporting ligament, grows and builds itself up in love, as each part does its work.
> (Ephesians 4:14–16)

Jesus prepared and equipped His disciples as a foundation for His church. God still appoints leaders to prepare His people for service. The church becomes Christlike in its fellowship of service as it is nurtured in God's will and purpose by Bible-believing, Bible-following leaders.

Christlike in its Consecrated Commitment

Purity—holiness—must characterize the church if it is to be Christlike. But there is a further essential to holiness: sanctification, or what we will term consecrated commitment. Without such consecration, the goal of Christlikeness is illusory.

For believers serious about the church, consecrated commitment to Christ is not optional. It is absolutely necessary if the church is to be Christlike. It is absolutely necessary if the church is to make its proclamation effective.

Consecrated commitment was an essential part of Simpson's "Deeper Life" message. Before Christ can be our Sanctifier, we must "offer [our] bodies as living sacrifices, holy and pleasing to God" (Romans 12:1). God accepts that unconditional offering, making it His. In a change of metaphor, we discover that even as Christ identified Himself with us in His crucifixion in order to bear our sins, so we were identified with Him in His death. So we "count [our]selves dead to sin but alive to God in Christ Jesus" (Romans 6:11). We "offer [our]selves to God, as those who have been brought from death to life; and offer the parts of [our] body to him as instruments of righteousness" (6:13). Death sets us free from sin; our voluntary consecration to God makes us "slaves to righteousness" (6:18).

As we saw in chapter 3, knowing Christ as personal Savior is one thing. Receiving Him as personal Sanctifier is quite another. He will rule only if we allow Him to. Only as we totally relinquish to him our human self-sufficiency, only as we identify with Him in an act of conscious surrender can we hope to appropriate the fullness of Christ by His Spirit in our lives.

This consecrated commitment of ourselves to Christ is essential to the "works of service" that God wants to develop within His church. Since all members are called to serve, the whole church needs this equipping. Jesus established the pattern with His disciples as Word was translated into deed through them. Pastor-teachers need prepared and equipped elders and church leaders to assist them in teaching, guiding and administrating the church. These in turn prepare and equip the entire church to utilize its gifts to build up the members and to minister the gospel to the world.

In all its teaching ministries, the church, above all institutions, should strive for excellence, beginning with adults and extending to all age levels. Strange, is it not, that church schools are often considered primarily for children? Fresh and continuous leadership from adults, both in the church and in the home, is most needed. But it can only be expected as the church continuously and perseveringly prepares leaders and equips them.

Paul's concern for the Ephesian church was lest, in an unguarded moment, "savage wolves . . . come in" among the flock, making their kill (Acts 20:29). Even among the elders, there would be some who would "arise and distort the truth in order to draw away disciples after them" (20:30).

Possibly at no time in history have believers been exposed to more false teaching than today. We must counteract the pressures and preoccupations that divert attention from divine truth. We must offset the mass media messages that are mesmerizing the religious public. When Christ returns, He expects to find the church in effective service. The church's work is never burdensome when done in consecrated commitment and undergirded by the joy and strength Christ Jesus provides.

Preaching, teaching, training and serving must be integrated into the goals and objectives of the church. This will motivate learning (discipleship) and strengthen conviction (service). Faith connected with works is alive as surely as faith apart from works is dead (James 2:14). J.B. Phillips translates Second Timothy 3:16–17 in these words: "All scripture is inspired by God and is useful for teaching the faith and correcting error, for resetting the direction of a man's life and training him in good living. The scriptures are the comprehensive equipment of the man of God, and fit him fully for all branches of his work." The phrase "all branches of his work" includes every vocation, whether in the home, the church or the world of business and labor.

The church is the body of Christ, a composite of people organically related so that both laity and clergy share their spiritual gifts in service to Christ within a particular church. The New Testament envisions the local church as a center for recruiting, teaching and training workers to build up His church and further His kingdom as they move out into the world. In fact, the major outreach ministry of the church comes through the laity properly equipped and deployed for works of service. The church is Christlike in its consecrated commitment to service.

Christlike in its Outreach

As we noted in an earlier chapter, Jesus came into the world "to seek and to save what was lost" (Luke 19:10). He came preaching the good news of God: "The time has come. . . . The kingdom of God is near. Repent and believe the good news!" (Mark 1:14–15). Jesus came to save humankind; Jesus came to announce His kingdom.

During His postresurrection days on earth, Jesus especially prepared His disciples to perpetuate His ministry on earth. He "opened their minds" to understand the Scriptures. They were to preach repentance and the forgiveness of sins in His name "to all nations, beginning at Jerusalem" (24:47).

The process would be through disciple-making: by baptizing those who believed the Good News and teaching them obedience (Matthew 28:19–20). It was a mission impossible but for one key provision: Jesus would be the Authority and the "Presence" to make it work.

Growth in the church, spiritual and numerical, is produced by Christ's presence. Only 120 people were in the Jerusalem upper room when the day of Pentecost began. But they were prepared people; they had learned from Jesus and they were "prayed up." Less than 12 hours later, the new-born church numbered not 120 but 3,000!

Nor was it a single day's event. It continued. As those who turned to Christ on the day of Pentecost "devoted themselves to the apostles' teaching and to the fellowship, to the breaking of bread and to prayer" (Acts 2:42). "The Lord added to their number daily those who were being saved" (2:47). The presence of the church in the world is indispensable to world evangelization.

A Spirit-filled, Christlike church is going to reach out in evangelism and missions. Member witness enlarges the local fellowship. And the church becomes a support system for the special messengers God calls into missionary outreach. God calls His disciples not only into a personal relationship with Himself but at the same time into a corporate relationship with one another to maximize their works of service.

Someone has observed that in the West we tend to confuse the words *personal* and *private*. Although our faith is personal, it was not intended to be private. For it to be most effective, faith needs to be related not only to Christ but to the organic church, Christ's body.

Jesus said, "You are the light of the world. A city on a hill cannot be hidden" (Matthew 5:14). He must have had in mind a city at night. The lonely, frightened wanderer in the night would see the beckoning lights of a town or city. "In the same way," Jesus adds, "let your light shine" (5:16). The world waits to see God-possessed, fire-lit saints who know how to show forth Christ Jesus, "the true light that gives light to every man" (John 1:9).

In his book *I Believe in the Church,* David Watson says:

> Both the proclamation and demonstration of the good news of Jesus Christ must be done not just by the individual, but by the church. The church that preaches the gospel must embody the gospel. The good news must be seen in our corporate relationships, worship, joy and life. With the steady erosion of relationships in today's world, the church needs urgently to become a visible community marked by love, God's new society in Christ. Unless renewal precedes evangelism, the credibility gap between what the church preaches and what the church is, will be too wide to be bridged. It is only when the world sees the living body of Christ on earth that it will be in any way convinced of the reality and relevance of Christ Himself.[3]

Evangelism and missions are not everything the church does. But they are the inevitable result of a maturing church prepared to follow Christ fully and to live in union with Him. Growth in spiritual maturity inevitably results in worship. Out of worship flow evangelism and missions. If the faith and vision of a church are clear, that church must share the privilege of knowing Christ and experiencing His authority and fullness. It was the vibrant church at Antioch that sent forth Barnabas and Paul. It was the enthusiastic church at Thessalonica that rang out the gospel in Macedonia and Achaia and "everywhere" (1 Thessalonians 1:8).

The church is more than God's means to evangelize our world, momentous though that is. The church shares the very nature of Christ. The church is the object of His special love. Christ "gave himself up for her to make her holy, cleansing her by the washing with water through the word, and to present her to himself as a radiant church, without stain or wrinkle or any other blemish, but holy and blameless" (Ephesians 5:25–27).

To believe in Christ and not love His church is an aberration. Christ awaits the day when the church will be His radiant, blemish-free bride. The church waits, too. And while this "bride" waits she works, confident that when Christ appears she will at last bear His likeness, for she will see Him as He is (1 John 3:2).

Christlike in its Hope of the Kingdom

A special outlook on the world and life itself colors and characterizes a Christlike church. *Jesus is returning!* That "blessed hope" (Titus 2:13) puts a gleam in the eye and a spring in the footstep of every Christ-committed, Spirit-filled believer. Jesus is returning to judge the world and to set up His kingdom of righteousness on earth!

This great anticipation of the coming kingdom is stated or implied in hundreds of Old Testament prophecies. It is explicitly detailed by Old Testament Daniel, by Paul in his Letters, by John in Revelation, and by Jesus Himself.

The premillennial return of Jesus Christ is a hope that rises like a mountain peak, giving reference to our direction in life and providing us substantive reason to press on. The kingdom of God is the divine rule given by God the Father to God the Son. It will come when Jesus Christ has subdued all enemies. Then "the kingdom of the world [will] become the kingdom of our Lord and of His Christ, / and he will reign for ever and ever" (Revelation 11:15). It is this kingdom that men must receive in childlike faith (Mark 10:15) or face destruction (John 3:17).

The kingdom is dynamic in power and supernatural in its working. It is altogether a sovereign work of God, although it operates in and through the church, which is an heir and coheir with Christ in that future glory and manifestation of His glory (Romans 8:17; Ephesians 1:23). Kingdom members will be rewarded according to the works of service they perform on earth (2 Corinthians 5:10). This kingdom is the believer's highest reward. It is to be sought first and foremost (Matthew 6:33).

The hope of Christ's kingdom kept the early church going amid the intense persecutions of the first three Christian centuries. Not until the fourth century, when Augustine associated the church with the visible kingdom of God and the city of God, did zeal for the kingdom begin to flag. But Augustine was wrong. The church is not the kingdom, although the relationship between the two is strong. The kingdom is first internal, through the proclamation of the gospel and the calling out of a people for God. When Christ returns to earth, the extent of the kingdom will at last become manifest.

The kingdom came into the world in the Person of Jesus Christ. It exists in the world through the church. When the church has preached the gospel of the kingdom in the whole world as a testimony to all nations, then the end will come (Matthew 24:14). Christ will return to establish His kingdom on earth and reward His church.

A Christ-like church has a kingdom outlook, a persevering motivation and a service focus that encompasses all of life, space and time. All of the church's service is rendered in the light of the Lord's return. Three significant principles regarding His return should rule the vision and motivation of the whole church:

1. The same Jesus who lived a physical life on earth is return-ing to restore fully the kingdom to the Father. The Jesus who is returning is the Jesus who endured the trials and temptations of human life, who ministered the truth of God in perfect servanthood, who gave His sinless life as a ransom for sinful man, who rose again and ascended to the Father's right hand.

This truth is a bold challenge to the existential mind-set of today that supposes meaning—if, indeed, there is any meaning—is comprised of the present, the world as it now exists. The reality of Christ goes beyond philosophi-cal and religious theory. His existence is rock-firm truth. The Christ who created the world and now sustains it provides meaning for human life and ample provision for its fulfillment. And He is returning! (Acts 1:11).

To a cynical world, the return of Christ is unbelievable. To the faint-hearted believer, it is mind-boggling. To the consecrated, committed Christian, it is indeed the "blessed hope" and the "glorious appearing." Paul shares with the Thessalonian church how it will happen:

> *The Lord himself will come down from heaven, with a loud command, with the voice of the archangel and with the trumpet call of God, and the dead in Christ will rise first. After that, we who are still alive and left will be caught up with them in the clouds to meet the Lord in the air. And so we will be with the Lord forever. Therefore en-courage each other with these words.*
> (1 Thessalonians 4:16–18)

2. The premillennial coming of Christ provides a solid founda-tion for faith. Creation itself, affected by sin and in "the bondage to decay, . . . has been groaning as in the pains of childbirth right up to the present time" (Romans 8:21–22). Although Satan has usurped authority as the god of this world, he will be unseated and punished everlastingly (Revelation 20:10). Heaven and earth will be reconciled (Colossians 1:20).

This is our Father's world, and He is eager for the church to occupy it. No wonder "creation waits in eager expectation for the sons of God to be revealed" (Romans 8:19)! No wonder "we ourselves, who have the firstfruits of the Spirit, groan inwardly as we wait eagerly for our adoption as sons, the redemption of our bodies. For in this hope we were saved" (8:23–24)!

Creation's eagerness and our eagerness rise in crescendo with the present concerns over ecology and the ozone depletion. With proliferating wars and rumors of wars, with politicians speaking of a new world order, with earthquakes, famine and pestilence wreaking their havoc, believers lift up their heads. Their redemption draws near (Luke 21:28)! They know their faith and service are grounded in bedrock reality. Christ is coming for His church to usher in a millennium of peace on earth![4]

3. Hope in the premillennial return of Christ causes believers to invest themselves in the church's Christlikeness and its obedience to the Great Commission. Christ is coming again for His church. The Bridegroom is coming for His bride.

The Bible paints a somber picture of conditions just preceding Christ's return. The conflict of the ages will sharpen (1 Timothy 4:1–3; 2 Timothy 3:1–4). World wickedness will escalate (2 Thessalonians 2:8–12). Men will faint from terror (Luke 21:26).

Will Christ return for His church before the great tribulation He predicted? Many dispensational fundamentalists believe He will. Simpson held that His return would precede the final three and a half years of intense tribulation. Many find biblical support for their view that the church will *not* be spared from the tribulation. A.W. Tozer observed: "You don't have to be technical and dogmatic and unbending about the second coming of Christ. Frankly, I think we have spoiled the hope of Christ's coming by a lot of unyielding charts and lines and circles in our prophetic teaching during the first half of the twentieth century." [5]

Paul confesses, "We know in part" (1 Corinthians 13:9). We may not have the sequence fine-tuned, but the certainty of Christ's return is not open to debate. We must not permit disagreement on the details to cloud the fact that Jesus *is* returning. And standing in the forefront of this climactic event is the church of Jesus Christ. He *will* come for His church (John 14:3; Acts 1:11), and He will reward it according to its faithfulness (2 Corinthians 5:10).

Christ's appointment as Head over everything for the church (Ephesians 1:22) is yet to have a dramatic fulfillment. For now the church is to exercise its Christ-given authority in proclamation and works of service. The most challenging time for the church could be in the days just prior to Christ's return. Paul assures the Romans: "If we are children, then we are heirs—heirs of God and co-heirs with Christ, if indeed we share in his sufferings in order that we may also share in his glory" (Romans 8:17).

Whether the suffering comes during the Great Tribulation (as some suspect) or in the course of confronting a hostile world and an angry devil, the promise is bright: If the church shares in Christ's sufferings, the church will also share Christ's glory. Perhaps the church's greatest glory will be to at last reflect the likeness of her Husband-Redeemer, King of kings, Lord of lords.

Endnotes

[1] A.B. Simpson, "The Secret of the Christian Life," *The Alliance Weekly* (June 27, 1925), p. 439.

[2] The Hebrew year was divided into 12 months; the day into 12 hours (Hebrew nights consisted of four "watches"). The 12 sons of Israel became 12 tribes comprising God's chosen people.

The 12 apostles chosen by Christ became the foundation (together with Old Testament prophets) of the church (Ephesians 4:20). The apostles' duties were preaching, teaching and administration. They were responsible for the life and welfare of the church community. This work eventually became the responsibility of the elders, though in a restricted sense from that of the Twelve. The number 12 consistently is associated with God's elective purpose of redemption and appears again with that association in Revelation.

[3]David Watson, *I Believe in the Church* (Grand Rapids: Wm. B. Eerdmans Publishing Co., 1978), pp. 17–18.

[4]NASA's $100 million project called NASA SETI (Search for Extra-Terrestrial Intelligence) is termed "one of mankind's most compelling questions" in an article entitled "Is Anybody Out There?" *Life* magazine (September 1992), p. 62. Man searches for what Scripture reveals.

[5]A.W. Tozer, *The Tozer Pulpit*, Gerald B. Smith, ed., vol. 3 (Harrisburg: Christian Publications, 1979), p. 150.

The Members of the Church

As proclamation is primarily the preaching of the Word and its "enfleshment" in the body-life of the church, so the priesthood of the believer and its expression of ministry are primarily effective through the members of the church. Local church members are a corporate "temple" where each one ministers as priest. Priestly ministry, performed with both responsibility and accountability, has a particular identity.

That being so, church membership is much more than a casual formality providing certain privileges or fulfilling certain regulatory functions. Jointly and equally, all members within the church are servant-ministers: "You also, like living stones, are being built into a spiritual house to be a holy priesthood, offering spiritual sacrifices acceptable to God through Jesus Christ" (1 Peter 2:5). A believer's priesthood is not above or beside a local church ministry; it is responsibly integrated within it. All members have "an anointing from the Holy One" (1 John 2:20). They are to offer living sacrifices of praise, prayer and good works (Hebrews 13:15–16).

The church provides a context for the believers' gifts, even though these gifts may extend the ministry of some members beyond the local church to other churches or to parachurch ministries. The church pastor exercises the same priesthood all the other members have. He administers his leadership gifts alongside and with the laity, but not in a way that displaces the gifts the members are to exercise. Healthy church growth demands that every member function in his or her divinely appointed ministry.

The priesthood of all believers was a critical issue of the Protestant Reformation. Since then, it has suffered much neglect. Under Old Testament Law, there was a hierarchy of high priest, chief priests, ordinary priests and Levites. Under Christ, priesthood extends to every believer. The church's priestly ministry is without rank, except in relation to the gifts the Holy Spirit gives by His sovereign determination.

The Members' Vocation

To the Corinthian church, Paul relates himself and Timothy (who was with him at the time and known to the Corinthians) as "God's fellow workers" (2 Corinthians 6:1). And he urges this church "not to receive God's grace in vain." The fact is, all believers are "fellow workers" involved in the task of ministering the grace of God to others. Unless they recognize and respond to their calling, they "receive God's grace in vain."

The Corinthian church had been nurtured by significant worker-leaders: Aquila and Priscilla (Acts 18:1–3), Silas and Timothy (18:5), Apollos (18:27–28) and Paul himself. There is indication that Peter may have ministered there, too (see 1 Corinthians 1:12). But Paul asks the Corinthian church to recognize these leaders in terms of the holistic servanthood of every member:

> *What, after all, is Apollos? And what is Paul? Only servants, through whom you came to believe—as the Lord has assigned to each his task. I planted the seed, Apollos watered it, but God made it grow. . . . Each will be rewarded according to his own labor. For we are God's fellow workers; you are God's field, God's building.*
> (1 Corinthians 3:5–9)

The bottom line is not the prestige of the farmer but what happens to the farm. The bottom line is not the eminence of the contractor but the quality of the temple he builds. God aims for ministry through a corporate priesthood. "So then, no more boasting about men! All things are yours, . . . and you are of Christ, and Christ is of God" (3:21, 32).

Peter makes a related comment in a text we looked at earlier: "As you come to [Christ], the living Stone—rejected by men, but chosen by God and precious to him—you also, like living stones, are being built into a spiritual house to be a holy priesthood, offering spiritual sacrifices acceptable to God through Jesus Christ" (1 Peter 2:4–5).

Not everyone can serve the Lord full-time as a missionary, a pastor or in some other related ministry. But all members are called to a ministry. They are not only to identify with a local church and there use their spiritual gifts, but most of them toil long hours for their livelihood and to support the Lord's work. That, too, is a part of their priesthood. For the dedicated Christian, vocation cannot be divided into sacred and secular; all of it is sacred.

In pursuing their daily livelihood, these members serve God in situations that often are hostile to Christianity. They meet people whom the professional pastors do not meet. Their vocation is a vital part of their priesthood.

But it must be church-related. Believers' ministries need an established home base. Their souls need to be nourished, their gifts affirmed, honed and integrated with the gifts of other members. There is a synergism of strength when people minister together, the gift of one complementing the gift of another. This biblical view of vocation has important implications for the building of Christ's church.

God's plan is to call His people to worship, to spiritual fellowship and to corporate service that glorifies Christ Jesus. Historically, it was God's direction to Israel: "You are to seek the place the LORD your God will choose from among all your tribes to put his Name there for his dwelling. To that place you must go; there bring your burnt offerings and sacrifices, your tithes and special gifts, what you have vowed to give and your freewill offerings, and the firstborn of your herds and flocks" (Deuteronomy 12:5–6).

In this age of the church, God's instructions are strikingly similar: "Let us not give up meeting together, as some are in the habit of doing, but let us encourage one another—and all the more as you see the Day approaching" (Hebrews 10:25).

Church membership is not optional. But membership must be more than a signature on a piece of paper. From the Bible's perspective, membership is a call to corporate service. A church that loses sight of this will be a weak church. The believer who fails to recognize this cannot avoid pernicious spiritual damage.

Baptism and Church Membership

Baptism is a public declaration of a person's voluntary identification with Jesus Christ in death and resurrection. In death, because the cross was God's verdict on sin, and God made Jesus "to be sin for us" (2 Corinthians 5:21). In resurrection, because Christ rose from the dead never again to die. "Just as Christ was raised from the dead, . . . we too may live a new life" (Romans 6:4).

Paul tells the Colossians he "joyfully" gives thanks to God the Father for qualifying them to "share in the inheritance of the saints in the kingdom of light" (Colossians 1:12). He goes on to say that God "has rescued us from the dominion of darkness and brought us into the kingdom of the Son he loves, in whom we have redemption, the forgiveness of sins" (1:13–14). *That* is what baptism symbolizes.

Baptism seals the believer's testimony. It is recognition that the believer has membership in the body of Christ. In baptizing new believers, a church signifies the need for a regenerate membership. But then, just as a wedding normally follows an engagement, as a diploma normally follows a course of study, so church membership should normally follow baptism. Baptism is an open expression of faith in God's life-transforming work. The church is where instruction in the faith should then take place.

Baptism does not in and of itself save. It is not a substitute for true repentance and personal faith. Baptism is for believers. It symbolizes the believer's new birth. It is the first step on the road to discipleship with unashamed commitment to Christ and His church.

Baptism signals a new lifestyle. New Testament believers were first known as followers of the "Way" (Acts 9:2; 19:9, 23; 22:4; 24:14, 22). Christianity was counter-culture in its ethical and religious lifestyle. As adherents of an illegal religion, converts were pressured to recant and denounce their faith. But the act of baptism helped to seal their resolve. The Christians stood firm in the gospel.

As the church increased in number, persecution became more severe. Jesus anticipated this strenuous sifting process, and had made provision for it in His Great Commission (Matthew 28:18-20). As we have already seen, the imperative in His Commission was to make disciples. The church was to make disciples by two means: by baptizing and by instructing. The order is the order we observe in the New Testament. New believers were baptized at once (Acts 2:41; 8:12, 36–38; 9:18; 10:47; 16:15, 33). Then followed the instruction in the essentials of the faith.

Alas! A Low Priority

In time—probably after the New Testament era—the church began to reverse the order, instructing new converts regarding the basis of their faith before baptizing them. The instruction for the *catechumenoi* or, in modern English, catechumens was a part of worship in the church. Until new converts evidenced an informed and steadfast faith, they were neither baptized nor permitted to join in the Lord's Supper at the conclusion of the worship service.

Today the evangelical church as a whole puts a low priority on both baptism and instruction—to its undoing. What Jesus stated to be supremely important to the making of disciples the evangelical church in practice has downplayed.

Under the leadership of Paul and Barnabas, the Antioch, Syria, church was a maturing congregation in a year's time. No other church except the one at Jerusalem was as intimately connected with the beginning of Christianity. Its voluntary financial assistance to the mother church in Jerusalem, whose members were suffering from famine (Acts 11:19, 27–30), is evidence of its vibrant nature.

Baptism helps assure right beginnings. Psychologists claim that a child learns more in the first two years than he or she will learn in all the years after that. Before age five, his or her personality traits are clearly entrenched. Family influences and a constructive environment are crucial to a child's well-being. In the spiritual realm, too, a loving church family will nurture the new convert. Relationships with those who walk close to God open new believers to the power and fullness of Christ the Lord. Missionary enthusiasm and dedication challenge new disciples to personal involvement in evangelism. Again, as the church balances the centripetal and centrifugal attitudes we discussed in chapter 5, new believers will move toward maturity in worship and ministry.

Baptism is not a one-time confession. Baptism, as Simpson believed, is the initiation into a lifetime of consecrated, Spirit-filled worship and service. God desires His children to experience the full meaning of their identification with Jesus in His death and resurrection. Then, in turn, we shall share the glory of the ministry Christ gives us, and ultimately be coheirs with Jesus for all of eternity.

Membership and the Lord's Table

The bedrock of Christianity is a personal and passionate devotion to Jesus Christ. For the believer who wishes to walk with God and demonstrate a commitment at once spiritual and practical, church membership is essential. Some of the members of that local church may be far from perfect. But true devotion to Jesus Christ demands both a personal and corporate responsibility for building His church and extending God's kingdom.

It is hard, if not impossible, to build a church without instruction. That is why Jesus, in His foreknowledge and wisdom, gifted us with pastors and teachers. Just as a contractor is necessary to the construction of a building, so spiritual leaders are important if the rank and file workers are going to build a spiritual church.

Everything a church does in serving Christ emanates from the incarnate, sinless life of Christ Jesus. He is available to us now through His death and resurrection. The bread and the cup of the Lord's Table symbolize His essential provision for His church: His body and His blood. Believers live in relationship to Christ and to each other on the basis of what Christ Jesus is for us, in us and through us. At the Lord's Table believers are confronted with the possibility of sins that have hindered both vertical and horizontal relationships. Because Christ graciously forgives us, we in turn are prompted to forgive those who sin against us. At the Lord's Table reconciliation and fellowship are affirmed. At the Lord's Table we implore the continued help of our High Priest who lives to intercede for us (Hebrews 7:25).

The Lord's Table is a periodic reminder that Jesus loves us. He loved us enough to live as a Servant among us. He loved us enough to lay down His life in sacrifice for the sins we had no way of erasing. Believers who at the Lord's Table remember Jesus' servanthood will find their own service and stewardship more and more fulfilling.

The Lord's Table is a reminder that Christ is at the church's center. Some churches make spiritual gifts central. Some put a particular experience in center place. For still others, it is church growth or a super Sunday school. Christ is at the church's center. When He is not, we are missing the point.

The Lord's Table is a reminder of our servanthood. In that upper room on that fateful eve of the crucifixion, Jesus served. Unless the church seeks to emulate Christ's attitude of service, all else it does will become a self-seeking charade.

The Lord's Table is a reminder that God's work demands team players. Paul begins his letter to the Philippians by addressing "all the saints in Christ at Philippi, together with the overseers and deacons" (Philippians 1:1). Simpson once described his New York Gospel Tabernacle as "mainly" congregational, but with the "addition" of a presbyterian form of eldership. What he meant was that the church members served in team ministry with the elders. This pattern has generally continued in The Christian and Missionary Alliance. The church is not helped by lone rangers and individualists bent on promoting their own ideas and satisfying their own craving for authority.

On the other hand, the church is not a democracy, guided by majority rule. A team of spiritual elder-leaders works together to shepherd the congregation into paths of prayer, faith and action. Biblical teaching and preaching equip the saints for mature spiritual service.

Kingdom-Living Members

George Hormel, founder of the well-known meat packing industry in Austin, Minnesota, that bears his name, once attended a prestigious business convention. During the lunch break, a stodgy business tycoon, puffing at a cigar, approached Mr. Hormel. Clearing his throat, the man asked, "And you, sir! What is your business?"

"My business," Hormel replied humbly, "is to be a Christian. But I pack pork to pay the expenses."

Being a Christian should be every Christian's primary business. The church is an investment house for the most important enterprise under heaven, the kingdom of God. No committed Christian is satisfied with a church that does not expect growth in spiritual character and in numbers. Progress is fundamental to any organism. When it stops growing, it begins to die. The church is no exception.

The letter to the Hebrews exhorts Hebrew Christians:

> *Therefore let us leave the elementary teachings about Christ and go on to maturity, not laying again the foundation of repentance from acts that lead to death, and of faith in God, instruction about baptisms, the laying on of hands, the resurrection of the dead, and eternal judgment. And God permitting, we will do so.*
>
> (Hebrews 6:1–3)

The church must have leaders who have heard the call of God to spiritual maturity—those who have gone beyond the elementary stage of spiritual development.

Potential leaders will be marked by close fellowship and camaraderie of interest in prayer, faith and vision with appropriate spiritual gifts. Those appointed to pastoral leadership are commissioned to be a shepherding team to build up the corporate church. Their main responsibility is to facilitate the worship of God, preparing God's people for works of service, in order to administrate a royal priesthood that seeks to model maturity in servanthood.

Members Who Pray

Prayer is sharing on earth Christ's enthronement in heaven in a most direct way. This ministry has a special significance for the corporate church. While a personal and devotional prayer life is basic, corporate prayer should be the church's first approach to extend Christ's kingdom at home and worldwide. Church membership includes sharing by corporate prayer the ministry of a royal priesthood in union with the intercessory ministry of our High Priest, Jesus Christ. This ministry requires full commitment to the body of Christ as well as to Christ Himself. It is through the corporate church that Christ and the Holy Spirit minister in plan and purpose.

The believer's personal ministry will find its largest fulfillment within corporate body-life. This is expressed by Paul in his prayer for the Ephesians that we refer to again:

> For this reason I kneel before the Father, from whom his whole family in heaven and on earth derives its name. I pray that out of his glorious riches he may strengthen you with power through his Spirit in your inner being, so that Christ may dwell in your hearts through faith. And I pray that you, being rooted and established in love, may have power, together with all the saints, to grasp how wide and long and high and deep is the love of Christ, and to know this love that surpasses knowledge—that you may be filled to the measure of all the fullness of God.
> (Ephesians 3:14–19)

The apostle envisions the great resources and glorious riches through togetherness with all the saints. The grasp of this vision—in its fullness and strengthening power—is realized through a bond of love that is rooted and established in this togetherness. Paul concludes his letter with the admonition: "Be alert and always keep praying for all the saints" (6:18). In other words, grasp the comprehensive ministry the church can have through its saints, and keep praying for them!

Prayer is the church's most important ministry. Only the ministry of the Word comes close. The whole church needs to be exercised in mutual concern and faith before God's throne. The strength of the congregation is not necessarily in numbers but in its faithfulness to Christ and to each other in prayer. No higher service can be rendered than in prayer and intercession. This service forms a bond in fellowship and Christian love that knows no equal. It is reminiscent of the familiar old stanzas:

> Blest be the tie that binds
>   Our hearts in Christian love;
> The fellowship of kindred minds
>   Is like to that above.
>
> Before our Father's throne
>   We pour our ardent prayers;
> Our fears, our hopes, our aims are one,
>   Our comforts and our cares.
>   —John Fawcett

Faith has its highest reward in corporate prayer. This the book of Acts demonstrates time and again. Arnold L. Cook, president of The Christian and Missionary Alliance in Canada, has voiced his observation regarding the felt need of revival. Dr. Cook says:

> We would like to legislate revival at our district conferences or general assemblies. The motion would

carry easily, but nothing would happen. There is one thing we can do: Pray. The one thing we know about revival is that it is always preceded by fervent prayer.[1]

When a horizontal relationship within the body of Christ corresponds to a passionate vertical relationship with Christ, there is tremendous power in our praying. Revival is always—*always*—preceded by fervent prayer.

Members and Their Spiritual Gifts

Gifts of the Spirit are not for selfish aggrandizement or to gain spiritual advantage. They are for service within the church body. No one can read First Corinthians 12, Romans 12 or Ephesians 4 without realizing the deep significance gifts have within the body of Christ. The Head of the church has distributed gifts and given leaders to the church in order that His body might be built up and its members equipped for works of service. Sometimes gifts need to be discovered. Usually they must be developed for greatest service.

The church runs two risks: One, the few members with great gifts will fail to utilize them. Two, the many members with lesser gifts will bury them. The second of these risks is the greater.

Spiritual gifts complement each other. The composite becomes a rich blend resulting in vigorous ministry. The greater or stronger gifts are most valuable when they bring many other gifts into ministry. The mission of the church is to cultivate every gift for fullest participation. The Scriptures make the point that the church's least noted and weakest member may be one of the most necessary (1 Corinthians 12:22–23). Discerning his or her gift and investing it well for the whole body is the responsibility of every member. But the wise church will seek out the best gifts and position them for stronger and wider service (12:31).

The Members' Time and Money

In the work of the kingdom, time can be more precious than money. Money is valuable only as it adds value to the time God grants us for service. In God's righteous judgment each person will be rewarded according to what he or she has done in the body (Romans 2:6; 2 Corinthians 5:10).

Money has tremendous possibilities, depending on how it is used and with what amount of time it is invested. Jesus spoke more often about money and its rightful use than about most other things. Our use of money clearly demonstrates our system of values and our commitment to God's service.

The Old Testament tithes and offerings represented a discipline that continued into the church era as members responded generously to the grace of God. "Mission" churches, hearing of the financial straits of Christians in Jerusalem, began a fund to help them. Paul instructs the Corinthians: "Do what I told the Galatian churches to do. On the first day of every week, each one of you should set aside a sum of money in keeping with his income, saving it up, so that when I come no collections will have to be made" (1 Corinthians 16:1–2).

Paul would later lay down general principles that continue to guide members of the church of Jesus Christ in their financial giving:

> *Remember this: Whoever sows sparingly will also reap sparingly, and whoever sows generously will also reap generously. Each man should give what he has decided in his heart to give, not reluctantly or under compulsion, for God loves a cheerful giver. And God is able to make all grace abound to you, so that in all things at all times, having all that you need, you will abound in every good work. As it is written:*

> *"He has scattered abroad his gifts to the poor;*
> *his righteousness endures forever."*

> *Now he who supplies seed to the sower and bread for food*
> *will also supply and increase your store of seed and will*
> *enlarge the harvest of your righteousness. You will be*
> *made rich in every way so that you can be generous on*
> *every occasion, and through us your generosity will result*
> *in thanksgiving to God.*
> (2 Corinthians 9:6–11)

Some people are able to invest more of their time than others in direct service to the church. Others have the means to invest more money. In both cases, as Jesus commented, "Where your treasure is, there your heart will be also" (Matthew 6:21). Time is money, and money represents the time it took to earn it. If the church is to be built up, valuable time spent in the Lord's work is absolutely necessary; money is no substitute. *Both* time and money are essential to the Lord's service.

Members in Creative Enterprise

Ritual and routine can be deadly to the church, the Lord's body, and every effort is needed to make room for creative enterprise. The world economy has been profoundly affected by modern technology and computerized efficiency. Industry, just to survive the intense competition, has trimmed middle management and challenged each employee to work as creatively as possible for the success of the total operation.

Actually, industry has rediscovered a New Testament principle. Jesus told His disciples:

> *"You know that those who are regarded as rulers of the*
> *Gentiles lord it over them, and their high officials exercise*
> *authority over them. Not so with you. Instead, whoever*
> *wants to become great among you must be your servant,*
> *and whoever wants to be first must be slave of all. For*

even the Son of Man did not come to be served, but to serve
and to give his life as a ransom for many.
(Mark 10:42–45)

For too long, industry operated on the assumption that
only the managers and company officers had intelligence.
The rank and file workers were know-nothing automatons
good only for repetitive-motion jobs. Now that industry is
adopting the team approach, it is discovering creative
talent within the rank-and-file that it never supposed was
there. So in the church. The greatness about the spiritual
gifts is the fact that every Spirit-filled believer has one or
more. The task of leaders is to help those who have been
sitting on the sidelines to discover these latent gifts and
become players on the team.

Needed: Faith and Vision

Handling divisive human issues and getting people to
work in unity demand creative abilities as well as faith
and vision. The presence of Christ through His Holy Spirit
will facilitate these tasks. Peter warns church leaders
against "lording it over those entrusted to you" (1 Peter
5:3). Rather, they are to be servants of the flock and examples to them. In the service of God's kingdom there are
no little people. Membership in the church gives opportunity to everyone for creative enterprise. The Head of the
church provides many gifts to His church and the riches
of His grace to build synergistic relationships. He desires
His people to be free from the we've-always-done-it-this-
way-before syndrome and make His church instead an expression of divine creativity.

Leadership teams—senior pastor, associate pastor, youth
pastor, director of Christian education, minister of music,
resident and supported missionaries, elders, deacons,
deaconesses—are appointed and commissioned as a fellowship of models and guides for true worship and service. As the church observes the integration of their
respective ministries, the whole church body is enriched.

241

How the corporate church recognizes these core qualities of its leaders becomes very significant to its centripetal and centrifugal functioning. If the leaders are "lords," that attitude will filter down. If they are servants, they will set the image of Christ-like servanthood.

An atomic power plant can safely provide electric power to a city if its core rods are properly controlled. Improperly controlled, those same core rods threaten the city with deadly destruction. So within the core leadership of the church lies the potential for great blessing and profound harm. Among a church's leaders the attracting centripetal forces and the expanding centrifugal energies come into closest dynamic interplay. These leaders must transform their individualistic, selfish pursuits into self-giving and Christlike servanthood that will transmit the power of the gospel.

Perhaps the church's greatest tragedy has been its stunted power of imagination. Christ is preparing the church to be His bride. That perfected bride is to be co-heir with Jesus of *everything*. Jesus Christ offers the church freedom—freedom to repent, freedom to serve, freedom to overcome. He told the church in Laodicea: "Those whom I love I rebuke and discipline. So be earnest, and repent. . . . To him who overcomes, I will give the right to sit with me on my throne, just as I overcame and sat down with my Father on his throne. He who has an ear, let him hear what the Spirit says to the churches" (Revelation 3:19–22).

The church is God's centerpiece of history. It is the final treasure of all God's creative handiwork. The whole earth, presently groaning in travail because of sin's curse, will be cleansed by fire and renovated to become Christ's kingdom. It will be repopulated by those of every tribe and language and people and nation who have been saved by the blood of Jesus Christ, whose names are registered in the Lamb's book of life.

Now we know only in part, but what God has revealed about the place Jesus is preparing for His children and the other place that shall be the habitation of those who reject Him should stimulate our earnest quest to be among the overcomers. The gruesome destination of those who are lost is not likely to stir the church until it is convinced of the "eternal glory that far outweighs" its present "light and momentary troubles" (2 Corinthians 4:17).

God promises to make those whom Christ purchased with His blood "a kingdom and priests to serve our God, / and they will reign on the earth" (Revelation 5:10). We have but one life to live. We have but one life to invest for Christ and His kingdom. As believers, our "priesthood" has eternal dimensions, depending on our involvement with the church in the present world. What we sow in this life we shall reap in the life to come. The benediction and prayer of the psalmist is this:

> *May God be gracious to us and bless us*
> *and make his face shine upon us,*
> *that your ways may be known on earth,*
> *your salvation among all nations.*
> (Psalm 67:1–2)

How the church sees itself and forms its life as a reflection of Jesus Christ through the help of God's grace has universal implications and eternal significance for God's kingdom.

General William Booth, founder of the Salvation Army, once said he wished he could send his recruits to heaven for five minutes and then to hell for five minutes. He believed the experience would transform them into an elite corps of evangelists. Undoubtedly a first-hand experience of such contrast would drastically change our perception of "such a great salvation" (Hebrews 2:3). But this would not compare with the contrast Jesus experienced when He freely left heaven's glory and became the God-Man in order that we might become like Him and share His reign in His kingdom.

243

Jesus Christ wants to be not only our Savior but our Sanctifier that He might enlarge our capacity to share His beauty and likeness for eternity. This should be the consuming desire of all the church, the bride of Christ. Members who live for His coming with firm expectation will echo the prayer of John as he completed Revelation:

"Amen. Come, Lord Jesus."

Endnote

[1] Arnold L. Cook, "What Is Our Future?" *Alliance Life* (April 28, 1993), p. 7.